NEW THINKING ABOUT
POLLUTION

21ST CENTURY SCIENCE

NEW THINKING ABOUT
POLLUTION

EDITED BY ROBERT CURLEY, MANAGER, SCIENCE AND TECHNOLOGY

Britannica®
Educational Publishing

IN ASSOCIATION WITH

ROSEN
EDUCATIONAL SERVICES

Published in 2011 by Britannica Educational Publishing
(a trademark of Encyclopædia Britannica, Inc.)
in association with Rosen Educational Services, LLC
29 East 21st Street, New York, NY 10010.

Distributed exclusively by Rosen Educational Services.
For a listing of additional Britannica Educational Publishing titles, call toll free (800) 237-9932.

First Edition

Britannica Educational Publishing
Michael I. Levy: Executive Editor
J.E. Luebering: Senior Manager
Marilyn L. Barton: Senior Coordinator, Production Control
Steven Bosco: Director, Editorial Technologies
Lisa S. Braucher: Senior Producer and Data Editor
Yvette Charboneau: Senior Copy Editor
Kathy Nakamura: Manager, Media Acquisition
Robert Curley, Manager, Science and Technology

Rosen Educational Services
Jeanne Nagle: Senior Editor
Nelson Sá: Art Director
Cindy Reiman: Photography Manager
Matthew Cauli: Designer, Cover Design
Introduction by Monique Vescia

Library of Congress Cataloging-in-Publication Data

New thinking about pollution/edited by Robert Curley.
    p. cm. — (21st century science)
"In association with Britannica Educational Publishing, Rosen Educational Services."
Includes bibliographical references and index.
ISBN 978-1-61530-135-5 (library binding)
1. Pollution. I. Curley, Robert, 1955-
TD174.N448 2011
628.5—dc22

2010009095

Manufactured in the United States of America

On the cover: © *www.istockphoto.com/Nicolas Loran (smokestack);* © *www.istockphoto.com/
dra_schwartz (background)*

On page 10: A young Filipino boy wades through plastics and other rubbish that has
accumulated in Manila Bay. *China Photos/Getty Images*

On page 18: Response crews battle an inferno aboard an oil rig off the U.S. Gulf Coast on
April 21, 2010. The resulting oil slick created an ecological disaster of tremendous proportions.
U.S. Coast Guard photo

On pages 5, 19, 30, 55, 72, 80, 114, 148, 188, 217, 255, 258, 260: © *www.istockphoto.com/
dra_schwartz*

CONTENTS

21

25

49

INTRODUCTION

In the eastern Pacific Ocean, midway between California and Hawaii, an enormous collection of plastic debris—bottle caps, old toothbrushes, cigarette lighters, and other refuse—floats in the water. Millions of tons of plastic from both coastal and inland cities around the entire Pacific Rim drift with the ocean currents, eventually massing in one giant eddy formally known as the North Pacific Subtropical Gyre. The accumulation of refuse in this particular gyre is estimated to be found in an area twice as large as the state of Texas—and the problem shows no sign of abating.

What some call the "Great Pacific Garbage Patch" serves as a dramatic reminder that pollution is an issue of enormous proportions. Not only that, but it also proves that the contamination of the world's air, land, and water does not respect national boundaries. Industrial smoke from factories in the developed world fouls the air in the Arctic. Mercury ingested by a fish netted off one coast will wind up on someone's dinner plate halfway around the world. Pollution is present all over Earth in various forms, posing a threat to the health of the planet and the life forms that inhabit it. The types of pollution, the danger they pose to humans and other creatures, and attempts to ameliorate or eradicate the problems they cause are the subject of this volume.

As a result of human activity such as the burning of fossil fuels, or even natural events such as forest fires and volcanic eruptions, certain by-products are dispersed into the air or wind up in soil and water. When the amount of these substances or excess energy outstrips Earth's ability to absorb or disperse them, the environment becomes polluted. Pollution has plagued the planet for centuries. Heaps of oyster shells and discarded stone tools mark the spots where ancient peoples made their camps. The world's first sewer, the Cloaca Maxima, funneled rain and waste from the streets of ancient Rome—and dumped them directly into the Tiber River. The air has been befouled as long as fossil fuels have been burned for heat and light, reaching new heights during the Industrial Revolution, with its belching factory smokestacks and machinery exhaust.

Pollution of all types is tied to population growth; the more people there are, the more pollutants they and their activities will produce. Since 1950, the number of people inhabiting Earth has sharply increased. Coinciding with the increase in population has been the introduction of new and more potentially dangerous types of pollutants, such as polychlorinated biphenyls (PCBs), dichlorodiphenyltrichloroethane (DDT) and other pesticides, and the chemical compounds used in the creation of plastics.

Rather than breaking down into harmless chemical components, these substances accumulate in the environment—and in the bodies of animals, including humans. Scientists have linked growing amounts of such pollutants to increased rates of birth defects, cancers, and other health problems. Sources of air pollution that pose a threat to human health include diesel engines, vehicular traffic, and steel mills. Tiny airborne particles, such as lead, are particularly dangerous, since lungs have the capacity to expel larger particles, whereas the smaller ones become trapped in the lower respiratory system.

In the early 1970s, scientists became concerned about a family of chemicals called chlorofluorocarbons (CFCs), used in air conditioners and refrigerators and as propellants in aerosol cans. Research indicated that CFCs destroy ozone molecules in the upper atmosphere, depleting the ozone layer that shields Earth from the Sun's ultraviolet radiation and exposing humans to a slew of harmful consequences, from sunburns to cancer. Fears over the effects of CFCs were confirmed when a large hole in the ozone layer was discovered over the Antarctic. Scientific evidence and public concern led to the Montreal Protocol of 1987, an international agreement to limit the production and use of CFCs.

Another threat to Earth's atmosphere is the buildup of gases such as carbon dioxide and methane. These particular pollutants are called "greenhouse gases" because they mimic the way glass windowpanes allow heat to be retained in a greenhouse. The gases absorb infrared radiation generated by Earth's surface after it has been warmed by sunlight and warms the atmosphere, which re-radiates infrared light back to the surface and results in more warming. From the start of the Industrial Revolution in the 18th century to the present day, the amount of carbon dioxide, methane, and other greenhouse gases in the atmosphere has increased at a faster rate than would be expected from normal climate change. Most scientists believe that the rising levels of greenhouse gases in the atmosphere are raising temperatures on the planet, which could disrupt weather patterns enough to cause, among other phenomena, rising sea levels and coastal flooding.

Yet another problem caused by airborne pollutants is acid rain. Automobiles, industrial refineries, and electric power plants send sulfur dioxide and nitrogen oxide emissions high into the air, where they mix with water vapour in clouds to form sulfuric and nitric acids. The acidic precipitation that falls from these clouds harms forests, fields, and aquatic plants and animals, and eats away at the marble and limestone in buildings and monuments.

Collecting and trapping particulates is a vital part of combating air pollution. New industrial smokestacks are in use, with scrubbers that limit both soot and sulfur dioxide. Innovative engine designs, such as those in hybrid vehicles, limit the amount and type of emissions that motor vehicles release into the atmosphere every day. These and other advances in air pollution technology, such as electrostatic precipitators and baghouse filters, have also helped reduce the number of airborne particles.

Vast amounts of domestic and industrial solid waste pollute the land. Some refuse is recycled and reused, but enormous quantities are buried in landfills, where great care must be taken to prevent the leaching of harmful chemicals into the soil. Some solid waste is burned inside incineration units. This method of disposal produces energy from waste, but it raises anew the problem of air pollution. In addition, a growing amount of material winding up in landfills is electronic waste. Discarded computers, televisions, cell phones, and other types of "e-waste" contain toxic substances such as mercury, lead, and cadmium.

For decades, before laws were passed that dictated safe industrial waste disposal practices, companies had disposed of highly toxic chemicals by dumping material in areas that were not meant to hold such dangerous waste. Sometimes the precaution of storing hazardous chemicals in containers was taken, but often the barrels were simply deposited in open-air dumping grounds. The waste did not stay contained forever. Eventually, barrels leaked, or materials were otherwise spilled, and the dangerous chemicals leached into the soil. Such was the case in Love Canal, a housing development near Niagara Falls, New York, that was built on the site of a chemical waste dump.

Hazardous waste has been the focus of large-scale cleanup efforts and government legislation. The first U.S. law to address the problem of toxic waste dumps was enacted in 1980, when Congress created the Superfund, an emergency fund for cleaning up hazardous waste disposal sites. Other methods of dealing with hazardous waste include safer modes of transportation and secure landfills.

While currently there is no federal mandate to recycle e-waste, many U.S. states have enacted e-waste laws, and consumers have become more informed about the hazards this type of refuse poses. Manufacturers have committed to building electronic devices in more environmentally responsible ways.

Clean water is essential to life, yet too many freshwater sources have been compromised. Industries have discharged chemicals directly into rivers and streams. In agricultural areas, animal waste, sediment, fertilizer, and pesticides run off from farms into local watersheds. Oceans are not immune to pollution, either. In addition to refuse-collecting gyres, oxygen-starved "dead zones" have developed where polluted waters discharge into the ocean. Scientists now believe that global warming is contributing to the expansion of these dead zones.

Other types of water pollution are, perhaps, less obvious than the sight of trash accumulating along shorelines, tremendous algae blooms in lakes, or oil slicks washing up onto shorelines. Excess heat, from power-plant cooling water, also is considered a pollutant, since it adversely affects aquatic life in rivers and lakes, as does eroded topsoil.

In order to make water fit for human use or consumption, it must be treated to reduce the presence of pollutants such as soil sediment and chemicals, as well as any microorganisms that may occur naturally in water sources such as lakes or reservoirs. When intended for drinking or bathing, water is put through a number of processes, including clarification, disinfection, filtration, and softening. Potable, or consumable, water can be derived from a saltwater source through desalination processes.

Various treatment methods are required to combat pollution caused by sewage as well. Also called wastewater, sewage is water that has been contaminated by use in homes or industry and is discharged into sewers, which eventually may drain the sewage back into water sources such as rivers and oceans. Sewage treatment is accomplished by funneling wastewater from homes and storm drains to plants that filter out impurities. Depending on how the recovered water will be reused—for example, for human consumption or for watering lawns and irrigating fields—sewage may pass through several treatment levels.

Another form of pollution that increasingly impacts the quality of life on Earth is noise pollution. The clamour of air traffic, moving vehicles, and building construction blocks out the sounds of nature and can cause health problems ranging from stress and insomnia to deafness. The noise of ship engines, offshore drilling, and underwater sonar have adverse effects on marine animals. Light pollution also is a growing problem on this crowded planet. Urban centres generate so much light that city dwellers rarely see the stars at night. Artificial light can interfere with astronomical observations and disrupt animal behaviour, such as bird migrations and the nesting of endangered sea turtles. Ordinances in some coastal communities require residents to turn off beachfront lights.

Yet another potential type of pollution that has environmentalists—and ordinary citizens—concerned is radioactive waste. The development of nuclear weapons and nuclear power plants has produced radioactive waste, creating a hazardous new pollutant that takes thousands of years to decay. The 1986 explosion at the nuclear reactor in Chernobyl, Ukraine, and its aftermath served as a terrible reminder of the dangers of radiation exposure.

More than an environmental concern, global pollution is an economic issue. Large, prosperous nations such as the United States continue to generate disproportionate amounts of Earth's pollution. Citizens in these countries can easily get used to a comfortable and convenient lifestyle, and may resist having to change their habits to benefit

Mother Nature. Developing nations may be unwilling to limit their own growth for the sake of the environment, and undeveloped nations simply do not have the resources to do so. Additionally, regulations that might reduce profits are often resisted by businesses, the people whom they employ, and their political representatives.

Efforts to control pollution have given rise to new fields of study such as environmental engineering and environmental law. Under pressure from concerned citizens and environmental groups, state and federal governments have passed laws aimed at reducing pollution. Agreements between nations have also arisen in an attempt to combat pollution. The Kyoto Protocol is an international agreement first adopted in 1997 by 37 industrialized countries and the European Union (EU) that sets targets for reducing greenhouse gas emissions to 5 percent below 1990 levels by 2008-2012.

At present, pollution is a grim reality of life on Earth, and it is tempting to feel discouraged about the extent of the problem. However, the good news is that people have never been more aware of the hazards of pollution, or more committed to doing something about them.

CHAPTER 1
THE PROBLEM OF POLLUTION

Environmental pollution is the addition of any substance (solid, liquid, or gas) or any form of energy (such as heat, sound, or radioactivity) to the environment at a rate faster than it can be dispersed, diluted, decomposed, recycled, or stored in some harmless form. The major kinds of pollution (classified by environment) are air pollution, water pollution, and land pollution. Modern society is also concerned about specific types of pollutants, such as noise pollution, light pollution, plastic pollution, and radioactive waste.

Although environmental pollution can be caused by natural events such as forest fires and active volcanoes, use of the word *pollution* generally implies that the contaminants have an anthropogenic source—that is, a source created by human activities. Pollution has accompanied humankind ever since groups of people first congregated and remained for a long time in any one place. Indeed, ancient human settlements are frequently recognized by their pollutants—shell mounds and rubble heaps, for instance. Pollution was not a serious problem as long as there was enough space available for each individual or group. However, with the establishment of permanent settlements by great numbers of people, pollution became a problem, and it has remained one ever since.

Cities of ancient times were often noxious places, fouled by human wastes and debris. Beginning about 1000 CE, the use of coal for fuel caused considerable air pollution, and the conversion of coal to coke for iron smelting beginning in the 17th century exacerbated the problem. In Europe, from the Middle Ages well into the early modern era, unsanitary urban conditions favoured the outbreak of population-decimating epidemics of disease, from plague to cholera and typhoid fever. Through the 19th century, water and air pollution and the accumulation of solid wastes were largely problems of congested urban areas. But, with the rapid spread of industrialization and the growth of the human population to unprecedented levels, pollution became a universal problem.

POLLUTION IN ACTION

By the middle of the 20th century, an awareness of the need to protect air, water, and land environments from pollution had developed among the general public. In particular, the publication in 1962 of Rachel Carson's book *Silent Spring* focused attention on environmental damage caused by improper use of pesticides such as DDT and other persistent chemicals that accumulate in the food chain and disrupt the natural balance of ecosystems on a wide scale. Public attention was focused in a more dramatic fashion by spectacular and, in some cases, catastrophic human-made disasters, such as the Bhopal chemical release of 1984, the Chernobyl nuclear explosion of 1986, and the Exxon Valdez oil spill of 1989. The human species had reached the point where it could endanger itself and all other species by harming the global environment—a lesson brought home repeatedly by events or turning points in history that made it clear something had to be done.

In this chapter three such turning points are profiled: the great smogs of London and Los Angeles in 1952, the dire state of eastern European countries in the early 1990s, and the sudden rise of China as a world-class economic power and polluter.

The Great Smogs of 1952

In the second week of December 1952, a disastrous fog occurred in London. High levels of sulfur dioxide and particulate pollution (and probably also sulfuric acid) led to the deaths of more than 4,000 people during that week and over the subsequent three weeks. Many, but not all, of the victims already had chronic heart or lung disease. Prize cattle at an agricultural show also died in the same period as a result of the fog. This episode spurred renewed attention to the problem of air pollution, which had been intermittently considered in England since the 14th century. Indeed, the term *smog*, derived from the words *smoke* and *fog*, was probably first used in 1905 by H.A. Des Voeux to describe atmospheric conditions over many British towns. It was popularized in 1911 by Des Voeux's report to the Manchester Conference of the Smoke Abatement League of Great Britain on the more than 1,000 "smoke-fog" deaths that occurred in Glasgow and Edinburgh during the autumn of 1909.

Air pollution begins as emissions from sources such as industrial smokestacks. The pollutants released into the air may impact the respiratory health of people working in and living near such facilities. Photos.com/Jupiterimages

The great London smog of 1952 led to the passage of legislation banning open coal burning, the factor most responsible for the pollution. This form of pollution, which is still known as "London smog," is common in many cities using coal as heating fuel, and it is associated with excess mortality and increased prevalences of chronic bronchitis, respiratory tract infections in the young and old, and possibly lung cancer. Today many industrial cities have legislation restricting the use of specific fuels and mandating emission-control systems in factories.

Also in 1952, a different kind of air pollution was recognized for the first time in Los Angeles. The large number of automobiles in that city, together with the bright sunlight and frequently stagnant air, leads to the formation of photochemical smog, now also known as "Los Angeles smog." This type of smog formation begins with the emission of nitrogen oxide from automobiles during the morning rush hour. This is followed by the formation of nitrogen dioxide through oxygenation and, finally, through a complex series of reactions in the presence of hydrocarbons and sunlight, by the formation of ozone and peroxyacetyl nitrite and other irritant compounds. Eye irritation, chest irritation with cough, and possibly the exacerbation of asthma occur as a result. Ozone is the most irritant gas known. In controlled exposure studies, it reduces the ventilatory capability of healthy people in concentrations as low as 0.12 part per million. Such levels are commonly exceeded in many places, including Mexico City, Bangkok, and São Paulo, where there is a high automobile density and meteorologic conditions favour the formation of photochemical oxidants. Although acute episodes of communal air exposure leading to demonstrable mortality are unlikely, there is much concern over the long-term consequences of brief but repetitive exposures to oxidants and acidic aerosols. Such exposures are common in the lives of millions of people.

EASTERN EUROPE AT THE END OF THE COLD WAR

After the fall of the Berlin Wall in 1989 and the collapse of the Soviet Union in 1991, the countries of eastern Europe faced a crisis of modernization. Among the many problems they pondered were ways to clean up the environment, for at that time eastern Europe was arguably the most polluted region on Earth. From Poland to Romania and from the Czech Republic to Moldova, its skies were dirty, its rivers and lakes contaminated, and its soils so poisoned that in some places the crops were inedible. In the former East Germany, average levels of sulfur dioxide and particulates were many times those found in the United States. The town of Boxberg, with its lignite-burning power plant, emitted more sulfur dioxide annually than the total emissions of Denmark and Norway combined. Acid rain had damaged 35 percent of Hungary's forests, 50 percent of East Germany's, 73 percent of the former Czechoslovakia's, 78 percent of Bulgaria's, and 82 percent of Poland's. A third of the rivers in the Czech Republic and half of those in Slovakia no longer supported aquatic life. As much as 80 percent of Romania's river water was unfit for drinking. The Black Sea received so much chemical pollution, large amounts of it via the Danube and Dnieper rivers, that 90 percent of the sea was biologically dead.

All this environmental damage levied sizable health costs. In the dirtiest parts of eastern Europe, life expectancy was several years lower than in cleaner areas, and the incidence of cancer, reproductive problems, and other ailments was far higher. In Hungary 1 in 17 deaths was thought to be due to pollution. Lack of environmental safeguards and poor health care combined to reduce the average life expectancy in the former Soviet Union to less than 64 years. In several high-pollution areas of western Russia, 10–20 percent of children were born with environmentally related birth defects. Indeed, shortly before the Soviet Union's demise, the Kremlin admitted that 3.5 million square kilometres (1.35 million square miles), or 16 percent of the socialist republic's territory, were so polluted as to be a risk to human health. They were a risk to political health as well. Some of the 45 million people who were worst affected joined other protesters in making environmental degradation a catalyst for ending communist mismanagement.

China in the 21st Century

When China hosted the 2008 Olympic Games in Beijing, it was a far cry from the country that in the 1950s Swedish Nobel Prize-winning economist Gunnar Myrdal had predicted would remain mired in poverty. As the world's fourth largest economy and third largest trading country, China at the time had accounted for approximately 5 percent of the world's gross domestic product and had recently graduated in status to a middle-income country. The country supplied more than one-third of the world's steel, half of its cement, and about a third of its aluminum. China's achievements in poverty reduction, in terms of both scope and speed, were impressive; about 400 million people had been lifted from poverty. The standard of living for many Chinese was improving, which led to a widespread optimism that the government's goal of achieving an overall well-off, or *Xiaokang*, society was possible in the near future.

The figures that illustrated China's remarkable economic achievements, however, concealed huge

A traffic jam in Bejing. As of 2006 China recorded the most emissions of green-house gasses, and vehicle exhaust is one of the biggest factors attributing to that dubious honour. Teh Eng Koon/AFP/Getty Images

and outstanding challenges that, if neglected, could jeopardize those very same gains. Many local and foreign-development analysts agreed that China's unsustainable and reckless approach to growth was putting the country and the world on the brink of environmental catastrophe. By 2008 China consumed more coal than the United States, Europe, and Japan combined, and had surpassed the United States as the world's biggest emitter of greenhouse gases. Beijing was also the biggest emitter of sulfur dioxide, which contributes to acid rain. Chinese scholars blamed the increase in emissions on rapid economic growth and the fact that China relied on coal for 70 percent of its energy needs. More than 300,000 premature deaths annually were attributed to airborne pollution. The changing lifestyle of the increasing number of middle-class families also contributed to the problem. In Beijing alone, 1,000 new cars were added to the roads every day. Seven of the 10 most polluted cities in the world were located in China.

The United Nations' 2006 Human Development Report cited China's worsening water pollution and its failure to restrict heavy polluters. More than 300 million people lacked access to clean drinking water. About 60 percent of the water in China's seven major river systems was classified as being unsuitable for human contact, and more than one-third of industrial wastewater and two-thirds of municipal wastewater were released into waterways without any treatment. The Pearl River Delta and Yangtze River delta, two regions well developed owing to recent export-oriented growth, suffered from extensive contamination from heavy-metal and persistent organic pollutants.

China was beginning to realize, however, that its growth path was not cost-free. According to its own State Environmental Protection Administration, as well as the

World Bank, air and water pollution was costing China 5.8 percent of its gross domestic product. When the Chinese government in 2004 began setting targets for reducing energy use and cutting emissions, the idea of adopting a slower growth model and the predictions about the looming environmental disaster were not received with enthusiasm at first. Within a few years, however, targets had been established for shifting to renewable energy, employing energy conservation, and embracing emission-control schemes. The target was to produce 16 percent of energy needs from alternative fuels (hydro and other renewable sources) by 2020.

Beginning in 2008, shops throughout China were forbidden to supply free plastic shopping bags, and the production and sale of very thin plastic bags—those that were less than 0.025 millimeters (0.001 inch) thick—were banned. An air-pollution target of 245 "blue sky days" that had been set for Beijing for 2007 was achieved on Dec. 28, 2007, according to the Beijing Municipal Bureau of Environmental Protection. On March 1, 2008, in preparation for the Olympic Games, new car-emission standards, which were in line with those in the European Union, came into force in Beijing, the city of Tianjin, Shandong province, and Inner Mongolia. In addition, beginning in July the use of private cars in Beijing and Tianjin was restricted so that cars with odd or even license-plate numbers were allowed on the streets only on alternate days. During the Games one-third of Beijing's cars were taken off the streets and industrial activity was curtailed in order to satisfy the air-quality requirements of the International Olympic Committee. The dramatic improvement in air quality—a 50 percent reduction in air pollution—proved so popular with the citizens of Beijing that when the regulations ended September 20, the authorities introduced a set of milder restrictions for a trial period through April

CHAPTER 2
POLLUTION IN THE AIR

Clean, dry air consists primarily of nitrogen and oxygen—78 percent and 21 percent, respectively, by volume. The remaining 1 percent is a mixture of other gases, mostly argon (0.9 percent), along with trace (very small) amounts of carbon dioxide, methane, hydrogen, helium, and more. Water vapour is also a normal, though quite variable, component of the atmosphere, normally ranging from 0.01 to 4 percent by volume; under very humid conditions the moisture content of air may be as high as 5 percent.

This fundamental resource—a clean and safe atmosphere—is under constant assault by the release of various gases, finely divided solids, or finely dispersed liquid aerosols at rates that exceed the natural capacity of the environment to dissipate and dilute or absorb them. These substances may reach concentrations in the air that cause undesirable health, economic, or aesthetic effects.

CRITERIA POLLUTANTS

The gaseous air pollutants of primary concern in urban settings include sulfur dioxide, nitrogen dioxide, and carbon monoxide. These are emitted directly into the air from fossil fuels such as fuel oil, gasoline, and natural gas that are burned in power plants, automobiles, and other combustion sources. Ozone (a key component of smog) is also a gaseous pollutant. It forms in the atmosphere via complex chemical reactions occurring between nitrogen dioxide and various volatile organic compounds (e.g., gasoline vapours).

Airborne suspensions of extremely small solid or liquid particles called "particulates" (e.g., soot, dust, smokes, fumes, mists), especially those less than 10 micrometres (μm; millionths of a metre) in size, are significant air pollutants because of their very harmful effects on human health. They are emitted by various industrial processes, coal- or oil-burning power plants, residential heating systems, and automobiles. Lead fumes (airborne particulates less than 0.5 μm in size) are particularly toxic.

The six major air pollutants listed above have been designated by the U.S. Environmental Protection Agency (EPA) as "criteria" pollutants, meaning that the concentrations of these pollutants in the atmosphere are useful as indicators of overall air quality. Except for lead, criteria pollutants are emitted in industrialized countries at very high rates, typically measured in millions of tons per year. All except ozone are discharged directly into the atmosphere from a wide variety of sources. They are regulated primarily by establishing ambient air quality standards, which are maximum acceptable concentrations of each criteria pollutant in the atmosphere, regardless of its origin.

FINE PARTICULATES

Very small fragments of solid materials or liquid droplets suspended in air are called particulates. Except for airborne lead, which is treated as a separate category, they are characterized on the basis of size and phase (i.e., solid or liquid) rather than by chemical composition. For example, solid particulates between roughly 1 and 100 μm in diameter are called dust particles, whereas airborne solids less than 1 μm in diameter are called fumes.

The particulates of most concern with regard to their effects on human health are solids less than 10 μm in diameter, because they can be inhaled deep into the lungs and become trapped in the lower respiratory system. Certain particulates, such as asbestos fibres, are known carcinogens (cancer-causing agents), and many carbonaceous particulates—e.g., soot—are suspected of being carcinogenic. Major sources of particulate emissions include fossil-fuel power plants, manufacturing processes, fossil-fuel residential heating systems, and gasoline-powered vehicles.

Carbon Monoxide

Carbon monoxide (CO) is an odourless, invisible gas formed as a result of incomplete combustion. It is the most abundant of the criteria pollutants. Gasoline-powered highway vehicles are the primary source, although residential heating systems and certain industrial processes also emit significant amounts of this gas. Power plants emit relatively little CO because they are carefully designed and operated to maximize combustion efficiency. Exposure to CO can be acutely harmful since it readily displaces oxygen in the bloodstream, leading to asphyxiation at high enough concentrations and exposure times.

Sulfur Dioxide

A colourless gas with a sharp, choking odour, sulfur dioxide (SO_2) is formed during the combustion of coal or oil that contains sulfur as an impurity. Most SO_2 emissions come from power-generating plants; very little comes from mobile sources. This pungent gas can cause eye and throat irritation and harm lung tissue when inhaled. It also reacts with oxygen and water vapour in the air, forming a mist of sulfuric acid (H_2SO_4) that reaches the ground as a component of acid rain. Acid rain is believed to have harmed or destroyed fish and plant life in many thousands of lakes and streams in parts of Europe, the northeastern United States, southeastern Canada, and parts of China. It also causes corrosion of metals and deterioration of the exposed surfaces of buildings and public monuments.

Sulfurous smog, which is also called "London smog," results from a high concentration of sulfur oxides in the air and is caused by the use of sulfur-bearing fossil fuels, particularly coal. This type of smog is aggravated by dampness and a high concentration of suspended particulate matter in the air.

NITROGEN DIOXIDE

Of the several forms of nitrogen oxides, nitrogen dioxide (NO_2)—a pungent, irritating gas—is of most concern. It is known to cause pulmonary edema, an accumulation of excessive fluid in the lungs. NO_2 also reacts in the atmosphere to form nitric acid (HNO_3), contributing to the problem of acid rain. In addition, NO_2 plays a role in the formation of photochemical smog, a reddish brown haze that often is seen in many urban areas and that is created by sunlight-promoted reactions in the lower atmosphere.

Nitrogen oxides are formed when combustion temperatures are high enough to cause molecular nitrogen in the air to react with oxygen. Stationary sources such as coal-burning power plants are major contributors of this pollutant, although gasoline engines and other mobile sources are also significant.

OZONE

Ozone (O_3), a key component of photochemical smog (also known as "Los Angeles smog"), is formed by a complex reaction between NO_2 and hydrocarbons in the presence of sunlight. Ozone is a highly toxic gas and is considered to be a criteria pollutant in the troposphere — the lowermost layer of the atmosphere — but not in the upper atmosphere, where it occurs naturally and serves to block harmful ultraviolet rays from the Sun. Because NO_2 and hydrocarbons are emitted in significant quantities by motor vehicles, photochemical smog is common in cities (such as Los Angeles) where sunshine is ample and high-way traffic is heavy. Certain geographic features, such as mountains that impede air movement, and certain weather conditions, such as temperature inversions in the troposphere, contribute to the trapping of air pollutants. The resulting smog causes a light brownish coloration of the atmosphere, reduced visibility, plant damage, irritation of the eyes, and respiratory distress.

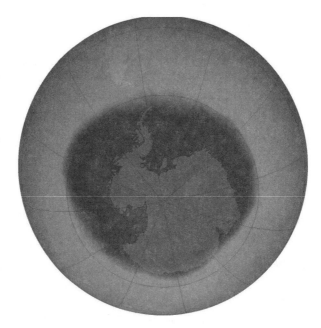

A 2005 image, created based on satellite data, showing what scientists say is a "hole" in the ozone layer over the Antarctic. NASA

LEAD

Inhaled particulates of lead (Pb) in the form of fumes and dusts are particularly harmful to children, in whom even slightly elevated levels of lead in the blood can cause learning disabilities, seizures, or even death. Sources of airborne lead particulates include oil refining, smelting, and other industrial activities. In the past, combustion of gasoline containing a lead-based antiknock additive called tetraethyl lead was a major source of lead particulates. In many countries there is now a complete ban on the use of lead in gasoline. In the United States, lead concentrations in outdoor air decreased more than 90 percent after the use of leaded gasoline was restricted in the mid-1970s and then completely banned in 1996.

AIR TOXICS

Hundreds of specific substances are considered hazardous when present in trace amounts in the air. These pollutants are called air toxics. Many of them cause genetic mutations or cancer, while some may have an adverse effect on brain tissue or fetal development. Although the total emissions and the number of sources of air toxics are small compared with those for criteria pollutants, these pollutants can pose an immediate health risk to exposed individuals and can cause other environmental problems.

Most air toxics are organic chemicals, comprising molecules that contain carbon, hydrogen, and other atoms. Many are volatile organic compounds (VOCs), organic compounds that readily evaporate. VOCs include pure hydrocarbons, partially oxidized hydrocarbons, and organic compounds containing chlorine, sulfur, or nitrogen. They are widely used as fuels (e.g., propane and gasoline), as paint thinners and solvents, and in the production of plastics. In addition to contributing to air toxicity and urban smog, some VOC emissions act as greenhouse gases (see below) and, in so doing, may be a cause of global warming. Some other air toxics are metals or compounds of metals—for example, mercury, arsenic, and cadmium.

In many countries, standards have been set to control industrial emissions of several air toxics. The first hazardous air pollutants regulated in the United States (outside the workplace environment) were arsenic, asbestos, benzene, beryllium, coke oven emissions, mercury, radionuclides (radioactive isotopes), and vinyl chloride. In 1990 this short list was expanded to include 189 substances. By the end of the 1990s, specific emission control standards were required in the United States for "major sources"—those that release more than 10 tons per year of any of these materials or more than 25 tons per year of any combination of them.

Air toxics may be released in sudden and catastrophic accidents rather than steadily and gradually from many sources. The risk of accidental release of very hazardous substances into the air is generally higher for people living in industrialized urban areas. Hundreds of such incidents occur each year, though none has been as severe as the Bhopal event, which has been called called the worst industrial accident in history.

Other than in cases of occupational exposure or accidental release, health threats from air toxics are greatest for people who live near large industrial facilities or in congested and polluted urban areas. Most major sources of air toxics are so-called point sources—that is, they have a specific location. Point sources include chemical plants, steel mills, oil refineries, and municipal waste incinerators. Hazardous air pollutants may be released when equipment leaks or when material is transferred, or they may be emitted from smokestacks. Municipal waste incinerators, for example, can emit hazardous levels of dioxins, formaldehyde, and other organic substances, as well as metals such as arsenic, beryllium, lead, and mercury. Nevertheless, proper combustion along with appropriate air pollution control devices can reduce emissions of these substances to acceptable levels.

Hazardous air pollutants also come from "area" sources, which are many smaller sources that release pollutants into the outdoor air in a defined area. Such sources include commercial dry-cleaning facilities, gasoline stations, small metal-plating operations, and woodstoves. Emission of air toxics from area sources are also regulated under some circumstances.

Small area sources account for about 25 percent of all emissions of air toxics. Major point sources account for another 20 percent. The rest—more than half of hazardous air-pollutant emissions—come from motor vehicles. For example, benzene, a component of gasoline, is released as unburned fuel or as fuel vapours, and formaldehyde is one of the by-products of incomplete combustion. Newer cars, however, have emission control devices that significantly reduce the release of air toxics.

GREENHOUSE GASES

Since the beginning of the Industrial Revolution in the mid-18th century, there has been an increase in levels of certain trace gases in the atmosphere. These gases, collectively called greenhouse gases, make up only a fraction of all atmospheric gases, but they have the property of absorbing infrared radiation (net heat energy) emitted from Earth's surface and reradiating it back to Earth's surface, thus contributing to the phenomenon known as the greenhouse effect. Carbon dioxide, methane, and water

THE BHOPAL DISASTER

On Dec. 3, 1984, about 45 tons of the dangerous gas methyl isocyanate escaped from an insecticide plant in the city of Bhopal, Madhya Pradesh state, India, that was owned by the Indian subsidiary of the American firm Union Carbide Corporation. The gas drifted over densely populated neighbourhoods around the plant, killing thousands of people immediately and creating a panic as tens of thousands of others attempted to flee Bhopal. The final death toll may never be known. According to the government of Madhya Pradesh state, the accident took an immediate toll of about 3,000 lives, though the Indian Council of Medical Research has estimated that as many as 10,000 people died within the first 72 hours. Over the following quarter-century, 15,000 to 25,000 are said to have died from effects of the poisoning. Some half a million survivors have suffered respiratory problems, eye irritation or blindness, and other maladies resulting from exposure to the toxic gas.

Investigations later established that substandard operating and safety procedures at the understaffed plant had led to the catastrophe. Suits for damages were brought against the company, and in 1989 India's Supreme Court ordered Union Carbide to pay $470 million in compensation to the victims of the accident. In 1998 the former factory site was turned over to the state of Madhya Pradesh. Two decades after the chemical leak, more than 400 tons of industrial waste were still present on the site. Soil and water contamination in the area was blamed for chronic health problems and high instances of birth defects in the area's inhabitants. In 2004 the Indian Supreme Court ordered the state to supply clean drinking water to the residents of Bhopal because of groundwater contamination.

. vapour are the most important greenhouse gases. To a lesser extent, surface-level ozone, nitrous oxides, and fluorinated gases also trap infrared radiation. Greenhouse gases have a profound effect on the energy budget of the Earth system.

A number of processes influence greenhouse gas concentrations. Some, such as tectonic activities, have operated at timescales of millions of years, whereas others, such as vegetation, soil, wetland, and ocean sources and sinks, operate at timescales of hundreds to thousands of years. Human activities—especially fossil-fuel combustion since the Industrial Revolution—are responsible for steady increases in atmospheric concentrations of various greenhouse gases, especially carbon dioxide, methane, ozone, and CFCs.

The effect of each greenhouse gas on Earth's climate depends on its chemical nature and its relative concentration in Earth's atmosphere. Some gases have a high capacity for absorbing infrared radiation or occur in significant quantities, whereas others have considerably lower capacities for absorption or occur only in trace amounts. The influence of a given greenhouse gas on the radiant energy impinging on Earth's surface is measured by its radiative forcing, a concept defined by the Intergovernmental Panel on Climate Change (IPCC). To understand the relative influence of each greenhouse gas, so-called forcing values (displayed in watts per square metre) calculated for the time period between 1750 and the present day are given below.

WATER VAPOUR

Water vapour is the most potent of the greenhouse gases in Earth's atmosphere, but its behaviour is fundamentally different from that of the other greenhouse gases. The

Global mean radiative forcings since 1750

radiative forcing types	radiative forcing values (W/m²)	spatial scale	level of scientific understanding
long-lived greenhouse gases	CO₂ — 1.66 [1.49 to 1.83]	global	high
	N₂O — halocarbons — 0.48 [0.43 to 0.53]		
	CH₄ — 0.16 [0.14 to 0.18]	global	high
	0.34 [0.31 to 0.37]		
ozone	stratospheric — tropospheric — −0.05 [−0.15 to 0.05]	continental to global	medium
	0.35 [0.25 to 0.65]		
stratospheric water vapour from CH₄	0.07 [0.02 to 0.12]	global	low
surface albedo	land use — black carbon on snow — −0.2 [−0.4 to 0.0]	local to continental	medium to low
	0.1 [0.0 to 0.2]		
total aerosol — direct effect	−0.5 [−0.9 to −0.1]	continental to global	medium to low
total aerosol — cloud albedo effect	−0.7 [−1.8 to −0.3]	continental to global	low
linear contrails	0.01 [0.003 to 0.03]	continental	low
solar irradiance	0.12 [0.06 to 0.30]	global	low
total net anthropogenic	1.6 [0.6 to 2.4]		

(anthropogenic) / (natural)

−2   −1   0   1   2   Source: Climate Change 2007: The Physical Science Basis, Summary for Policymakers, Intergovernmental Panel on Climate Change

Since 1750 the concentration of carbon dioxide and other greenhouse gases has increased in Earth's atmosphere. As a result of these and other factors, Earth's atmosphere retains more heat than in the past.

primary role of water vapour is not as a direct agent of radiative forcing but rather as a climate feedback—that is, as a response within the climate system that influences the system's continued activity. This distinction arises from the fact that the amount of water vapour in the atmosphere cannot, in general, be directly modified by human behaviour but is instead set by air temperatures. The warmer the surface, the greater the evaporation rate of water from the surface. As a result, increased evaporation leads to a greater concentration of water vapour in the lower atmosphere capable of absorbing infrared radiation and emitting it downward.

CARBON DIOXIDE

Carbon dioxide (CO_2) is considered a normal component of the atmosphere, and before the Industrial Revolution the average levels of this gas were about 280 parts per million (ppm). By the early 21st century the levels of CO_2 reached 384 ppm, and they continue to increase at a rate of almost 2 ppm per year. Many scientists think that CO_2 should be regulated as a pollutant—a position taken by the EPA in 2009 in a ruling that such regulations could be promulgated. International cooperation and agreements will be necessary to reduce CO_2 emissions worldwide.

Natural sources of atmospheric CO_2 include outgassing from volcanoes, the combustion and natural decay of organic matter, and respiration by aerobic (oxygen-using) organisms. These sources are balanced, on average, by a set of physical, chemical, or biological processes, called "sinks," that tend to remove CO_2 from the atmosphere. Significant natural sinks include terrestrial vegetation, which takes up CO_2 during the process of photosynthesis.

A number of oceanic processes also act as carbon sinks. One such process, called the "solubility pump," involves

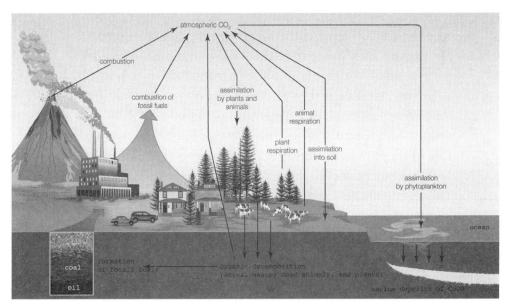

The generalized carbon cycle. Encyclopædia Britannica, Inc.

the descent of surface sea water containing dissolved CO_2. Another process, the "biological pump," involves the uptake of dissolved CO_2 by marine vegetation and phytoplankton (small, free-floating, photosynthetic organisms) living in the upper ocean or by other marine organisms that use CO_2 to build skeletons and other structures made of calcium carbonate ($CaCO_3$). As these organisms expire and fall to the ocean floor, the carbon they contain is transported downward and eventually buried at depth. A long-term balance between these natural sources and sinks leads to the background, or natural, level of CO_2 in the atmosphere.

In contrast, human activities increase atmospheric CO_2 levels primarily through the burning of fossil fuels (principally oil and coal, and secondarily natural gas, for use in transportation, heating, and the production of electricity) and through the production of cement. Other anthropogenic sources include the burning of forests and the clearing of land. Anthropogenic emissions currently account for the annual release of about 7 gigatons (7 billion tons) of carbon into the atmosphere. Anthropogenic emissions are equal to approximately 3 percent of the total emissions of CO_2 by natural sources, and this amplified carbon load from human activities far exceeds the offsetting capacity of natural sinks (by perhaps as much as 2–3 gigatons per year). CO_2 has consequently accumulated in the atmosphere at an average rate of 1.4 ppm by volume per year between 1959 and 2006, and this rate of accumulation has been uniform over time. However, certain current sinks, such as the oceans, could become sources in the future. This may lead to a situation in which the concentration of atmospheric CO_2 builds at an exponential rate.

The natural background level of carbon dioxide varies on timescales of millions of years due to slow changes in outgassing through volcanic activity. For example, roughly

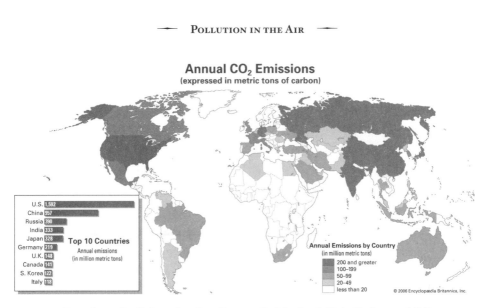

Encyclopaedia Britannica, Inc. Source: G. Marland, T.A. Boden, and R.J. Andres, Carbon Dioxide Information Analysis Center, Environmental Sciences Division, Oak Ridge National Laboratory, U.S. Department of Energy, Oak Ridge, Tennessee.

100 million years ago, during the Cretaceous Period, CO_2 concentrations appear to have been several times higher than today (perhaps close to 2,000 ppm). Over the past 700,000 years, CO_2 concentrations have varied over a far smaller range (between roughly 180 and 300 ppm) in association with the same Earth orbital effects linked to the coming and going of the ice ages of the Pleistocene epoch. By the early 21st century, CO_2 levels reached 384 ppm, which is approximately 37 percent above the natural background level of roughly 280 ppm that existed at the beginning of the Industrial Revolution. According to ice core measurements, this level (384 ppm) is believed to be the highest in at least 650,000 years.

Radiative forcing caused by carbon dioxide varies in an approximately logarithmic fashion with the concentration of that gas in the atmosphere. The logarithmic relationship occurs as the result of a saturation effect wherein it becomes increasingly difficult, as CO_2 concentrations increase, for additional CO_2 molecules to further influence the "infrared window" (a certain narrow band of wavelengths in the infrared region that is not absorbed by atmospheric gases). The logarithmic relationship predicts that the surface warming potential will rise by roughly the same amount for each doubling of CO_2 concentration. At current rates of fossil-fuel use, a doubling of CO_2 concentrations over preindustrial levels is expected to take place by the middle of the 21st century (when CO_2 concentrations are projected to reach 560 ppm). A doubling of CO_2 concentrations would represent an increase of roughly 4 watts per square metre of radiative forcing. Given typical estimates of "climate sensitivity" in the absence of any offsetting factors, this energy increase would lead to a warming of 2 to 5 °C (3.6 to 9 °F) over preindustrial times. The total radiative forcing by anthropogenic CO_2 emissions since the beginning of the industrial age is approximately 1.66 watts per square metre.

METHANE

Methane (CH_4) is the second most important greenhouse gas. CH_4 is more potent than CO_2 because the radiative forcing produced per molecule is greater. In addition, the infrared window is less saturated in the range of wavelengths of radiation absorbed by CH_4, so more molecules may fill in the region. However, CH_4 exists in far lower concentrations than CO_2 in the atmosphere, and its concentrations by volume in the atmosphere are generally measured in parts per billion (ppb) rather than ppm. CH_4 also has a considerably shorter residence time in the atmosphere than CO_2 (the residence time for CH_4 is roughly 10 years, compared with hundreds of years for CO_2).

Natural sources of methane include tropical and northern wetlands, methane-oxidizing bacteria that feed on organic material consumed by termites, volcanoes, seepage vents of the seafloor in regions rich with organic sediment, and methane hydrates trapped along the continental shelves of the oceans and in polar permafrost. The primary natural sink for methane is the atmosphere itself, as methane reacts readily with the hydroxyl radical (OH⁻) within the troposphere to form CO_2 and water vapour (H_2O). When CH_4 reaches the stratosphere, it is destroyed. Another natural sink is soil, where methane is oxidized by bacteria.

As with CO_2, human activity is increasing the CH_4 concentration faster than it can be offset by natural sinks. Anthropogenic sources currently account for approximately 70 percent of total annual emissions, leading to substantial increases in concentration over time. The major anthropogenic sources of atmospheric CH_4 are rice cultivation, livestock farming, the burning of coal and natural gas, the combustion of biomass, and the decomposition of organic matter in landfills. Future trends are particularly difficult to anticipate. This is in part due to an incomplete understanding of the climate feedbacks associated with CH_4 emissions. In addition, as human populations grow, it is difficult to predict how possible changes in livestock raising, rice cultivation, and energy utilization will influence CH_4 emissions.

Before the industrial age, levels of CH_4 in the atmosphere were approximately 700 ppb, whereas early 21st-century levels exceed 1,770 ppb. These concentrations are well above the natural levels observed for at least the past 650,000 years. The net radiative forcing by anthropogenic CH_4 emissions is approximately 0.5 watt per square metre—or roughly one-third the radiative forcing of CO_2.

SURFACE-LEVEL OZONE

The next most significant greenhouse gas is surface, or low-level, ozone (O_3). Surface O_3 is a result of air pollution;

it must be distinguished from naturally occurring strato-spheric O_3, which has a very different role in the planetary radiation balance. The primary natural source of surface O_3 is the subsidence of stratospheric O_3 from the upper atmosphere. In contrast, the primary anthropogenic source of surface O_3 is photochemical reactions involving the atmospheric pollutant carbon monoxide (CO). The best estimates of the concentration of surface O_3 are 50 ppb, and the net radiative forcing due to anthropogenic emissions of surface O_3 is approximately 0.35 watt per square metre.

NITROUS OXIDES AND FLUORINATED GASES

Additional trace gases produced by industrial activity that have greenhouse properties include nitrous oxide (N_2O) and fluorinated gases (halocarbons), the latter including sulfur hexafluoride, hydrofluorocarbons (HFCs), and per-fluorocarbons (PFCs). Nitrous oxide is responsible for 0.16 watt per square metre radiative forcing, while fluori-nated gases are collectively responsible for 0.34 watt per square metre. Nitrous oxides have small background con-centrations due to natural biological reactions in soil and water, whereas the fluorinated gases owe their existence almost entirely to industrial sources.

AIR POLLUTION
AND AIR MOVEMENT

Local air quality typically varies over time because of the effect of weather patterns. For example, air pollutants are diluted and dispersed in a horizontal direction by prevail-ing winds, and they are dispersed in a vertical direction by atmospheric instability. Unstable atmospheric conditions occur when air masses move naturally in a vertical direction, thereby mixing and dispersing pollutants. When there is little or no vertical movement of air (stable conditions), pollutants can accumulate near the ground and cause temporary but acute episodes of air pollution. With regard to air quality, unstable atmospheric conditions are preferable to stable conditions.

The degree of atmospheric instability depends on the temperature gradient (i.e., the rate at which air temperature changes with altitude). In the troposphere (the lowest layer of the atmosphere, where most weather occurs), air temperatures normally decrease as altitude increases; the faster the rate of decrease, the more unstable the atmosphere. Under certain conditions, however, a temporary "temperature inversion" may occur, during which time the air temperature increases with increasing altitude, and the atmosphere is very stable. Temperature inversions prevent the upward mixing and dispersion of pollutants and are the major cause of air pollution episodes.

Certain geographic conditions exacerbate the effect of inversions. For example, Los Angeles, situated on a plain on the Pacific coast of California and surrounded by mountains that block horizontal air motion, is particularly susceptible to the stagnation effects of inversions — hence the infamous Los Angeles smog. On the opposite coast of North America another metropolis, New York City, produces greater quantities of pollutants than does Los Angeles but has been spared major air pollution disasters because of favourable climatic and geographic circumstances.

THE GLOBAL REACH OF AIR POLLUTION

Because some air pollutants persist in the atmosphere and are carried long distances by winds, air pollution transcends local, regional, and continental boundaries, and it also may have an effect on global climate and weather. The problems of acid rain, stratospheric ozone, and global warming are compelling examples of how air pollution respects no nation's borders and often must be addressed through international cooperation.

Acid Rain

Acid rain has gained worldwide attention since the 1970s as a regional and even continental problem. Acid rain occurs when sulfur dioxide and nitrogen oxides combine with water vapour in the atmosphere, forming sulfuric acid and nitric acid mists. The resulting acidic precipitation (which falls not only as rain but also as snow, sleet, and hail) is damaging to water, forest, and soil resources. It has caused the disappearance of fish from many lakes in the Adirondack Mountains of North America, the widespread death of forests in mountains of Europe, and damage to tree growth in the United States and Canada.

The formation of acid rain generally begins with emissions into the atmosphere of sulfur dioxide and nitrogen oxide. These gases are released by automobiles, certain industrial operations (e.g., smelting and refining), and electric power plants that burn fossil fuels such as coal and oil. The gases combine with water vapour in clouds to form sulfuric and nitric acids. When precipitation falls from the clouds, it is highly acidic, having a pH value of about 5.6 or lower. (The pH scale ranges from 0 to 14, with lower numbers indicating increased acidity.) At several locations in the eastern United States and western Europe, pH values between 2 and 3 have been recorded. In areas such as Los Angeles, San Francisco, and Whiteface Mountain in New York, fog is often 10 or more times as acidic as the local precipitation.

Spruce trees damaged by acid rain in Karkonosze National Park, Poland.
Simon Fraser/Science Photo Library—Photo Researchers, Inc.

Precipitation and fog of high acidity contaminate lakes and streams, and are particularly harmful to fish and other aquatic life in regions with thin soil and granitic rock, which provide little buffering to acidic inputs. It also has been discovered that aluminum is leached from the soil in regions subjected to such acid precipitation, and that dissolved aluminum seems to be extremely toxic to aquatic organisms. All forms of acid precipitation have been found to damage various kinds of vegetation, including agricultural crops and trees, chiefly by inhibiting nitrogen fixation and leaching nutrients from foliage. In addition, these pollutants can corrode the external surfaces of buildings and other man-made structures; marble structures and statues are especially vulnerable to their damaging effects.

The problem of acid rain is not contained by political boundaries. Although this form of pollution is most severe in and around large urban and industrial areas, substantial amounts of acid precipitation may be transported great distances. For example, emissions from the burning of fossil fuels in the middle sections of the United States and Canada are precipitated as acid rain in the eastern regions of those countries, and acid rain in Norway comes largely from industrial areas in Great Britain and continental Europe. The international scope of the problem has led to the signing of international agreements on the limitation of sulfur and nitrogen oxide emissions. For instance, the Air Quality Agreement signed by the United States and Canada in 1991 has led to significant reductions in the emission of sulfur dioxide and nitrogen oxides in those two countries.

Stratospheric Ozone

Another global problem caused by air pollution is the depletion of ozone in the stratosphere. The ozone layer is a region of the atmosphere, roughly 15-48 km (9-30 miles) in altitude, that contains small quantities of ozone. Ozone is a form of oxygen that comprises three atoms (O_3) rather than the two atoms (O_2) found in ordinary molecular oxygen. In the troposphere, ozone is a pollutant, as described above in the chapters on criteria pollutants and global warming. However, at altitudes above 12 km (7 miles), ozone plays a crucial role in absorbing and thereby blocking ultraviolet (UV) radiation from the Sun before it reaches the ground. UV radiation is the cause of common sunburn, but long-term exposure to UV has been linked to skin cancer and other health problems.

In 1985 it was discovered that a large "ozone hole," an ozone-depleted region, is present every year between August and November over the continent of Antarctica. The size of this hole is increased by the presence in the atmosphere of CFCs, which emanate from aerosol spray cans, refrigerators, industrial solvents, and other sources and are transported to Antarctica by atmospheric circulation. Because it been demonstrated in the mid-1970s that CFCs posed a threat to the global ozone layer, the use of CFCs as propellants in aerosol cans was banned in the United States in 1978. Their use was subsequently restricted in several other countries. In 1987 representatives from more than 45 countries signed the Montreal Protocol, agreeing to place severe limitations on the production of CFCs.

GLOBAL WARMING

One of the most significant effects of air pollution is on climate change, particularly global warming. This is the phenomenon of increasing average air temperatures near the surface of Earth over the past one to two centuries, connected, in part, to the emission of greenhouse gases.

As a result of the growing worldwide consumption of fossil fuels, carbon dioxide levels in the atmosphere have increased steadily since 1900, and the rate of increase is accelerating. It has been estimated that if carbon dioxide levels are not reduced, average global air temperatures may rise another 4 °C (7.2 °F) by the end of the 21st century. Such a warming trend might cause melting of the polar ice caps, rising of the sea level, and flooding of the coastal areas of the world. Changes in precipitation patterns caused by global warming might have adverse effects on agriculture and forest ecosystems, and higher temperatures and humidity might increase the incidence of disease in humans and animals in some parts of the world.

Implementation of international agreements on reducing greenhouse gases are required to protect global air quality and to mitigate the effects of global warming. Global climate-change policy is guided by two major treaties: the United Nations Framework Convention on Climate Change (UNFCCC) of 1992 and the associated 1997 Kyoto Protocol to the UNFCCC (named after the city in Japan where it was concluded). In force since 2005, the Kyoto Protocol calls for reducing the emission of six greenhouse gases in 36 countries to 5.2 percent below 1990 levels in the "commitment period" of 2008–12. It has been widely hailed as the most significant environmental treaty ever negotiated.

INDOOR AIR POLLUTION

Health risks related to indoor air pollution have become an issue of concern because people generally spend most of their time indoors at home and at work. Indoor air pollutants include various combustion products from stoves, kerosene space heaters, and fireplaces, as well as volatile

A NOBEL FOR THE OZONE LAYER

The 1995 Nobel Prize for Chemistry was awarded to Paul Crutzen, a Dutch citizen with the Max Planck Institute for Chemistry, Mainz, Germany; F. Sherwood Rowland of the University of California, Irvine; and Mario Molina of the Massachusetts Institute of Technology. "By explaining the chemical mechanisms that affect the thickness of the ozone layer, the three researchers have contributed to our salvation from a global environmental problem that could have catastrophic consequences," the Royal Swedish Academy of Sciences said in its citation.

In 1970 Crutzen took some of the first steps in calling attention to the ozone layer's vulnerability. He showed that nitric oxide (NO) and nitrogen dioxide (NO_2) act as catalysts to speed decomposition of ozone (O_3). Those compounds form in the atmosphere from nitrous oxide (N_2O) released naturally at the surface by soil bacteria. A year later the U.S. scientist Harold Johnston warned that a planned fleet of commercial supersonic transport (SST) aircraft would release nitrogen oxides directly into the ozone layer and thus could damage it. Crutzen's and Johnston's work sparked strong debate among scientists and decision makers and marked the beginning of intensive research into the chemistry of the atmosphere.

The next major advance came in 1974, when Rowland and Molina showed that chlorofluorocarbons (CFCs), which were widely used as aerosol-spray propellants, air-conditioning refrigerants, and foaming agents in plastics manufacture, were transported to the ozone layer. There, under the influence of ultraviolet light, they participated in reactions that destroyed ozone molecules. Rowland and Molina wrote that continued use of CFCs would seriously deplete the ozone layer within decades. That prediction triggered strong scientific controversy. CFCs were a mainstay of modern society, and no substitutes were available. Chemists knew that CFCs were extremely nonreactive at the Earth's surface and thus believed that they posed no environmental threat. "Many were critical of Molina and Rowland's calculations, but yet more were seriously concerned by the possibility of a depleted ozone layer," the Swedish Academy said. "Today we know that they were right in all essentials."

organic compounds (VOCs) from household products (e.g., paints, cleaning agents, and pesticides). Formaldehyde off-gassing from building products (especially particle-board and plywood) and from dry-cleaned textiles can accumulate in indoor air. Bacteria, viruses, molds, animal dander, dust mites, and pollen are biological contaminants that can cause disease and other health problems, especially if they build up in and are spread by central heating or cooling systems. Environmental tobacco smoke, also called secondhand smoke, is an indoor air pollutant in many homes, despite widespread knowledge about the harmful effects of smoking. Secondhand smoke contains many carcinogenic compounds as well as strong irritants. In some geographic regions, naturally occurring radon, a radioactive gas, can seep from the ground into buildings and accumulate to harmful levels.

Exposure to all indoor air pollutants can be reduced by appropriate building construction and maintenance methods, limitations on pollutant sources, and provision of adequate ventilation. In some cases, however, the problem of indoor air pollution has been exacerbated by well-meaning efforts to lower air-exchange rates in buildings in order to conserve energy. Unfortunately, these efforts allow contaminants to accumulate indoors.

CHAPTER 3
AIR POLLUTION CONTROL

The best way to protect air quality is to reduce the emission of pollutants by changing to cleaner fuels and processes. Pollutants not eliminated in this way must be collected or trapped by appropriate air-cleaning devices as they are generated and before they can escape into the atmosphere. These devices are described in this chapter. The chapter begins by describing the technology that is designed to remove particulate and gaseous pollutants from the emissions of stationary sources, including power plants and industrial facilities. It concludes with a description of reducing emissions from the most ubiquitous mobile source on Earth, the automobile.

CONTROL OF PARTICULATES

Airborne particles can be removed from a polluted airstream by a variety of physical processes. Common types of equipment for collecting fine particulates include cyclones, scrubbers, electrostatic precipitators, and baghouse filters. Once collected, particulates adhere to each other, forming agglomerates that can readily be removed from the equipment and disposed of, usually in a landfill.

Because each air pollution control project is unique, it is usually not possible to decide in advance what the best type of particle-collection device (or combination of devices) will be; control systems must be designed on a case-by-case basis. Important particulate characteristics that influence the selection of collection devices include corrosivity, reactivity, shape, density, and especially size and size distribution (the range of different particle sizes in the airstream). Other design factors include airstream characteristics (e.g., pressure, temperature, and viscosity), flow rate, removal efficiency requirements, and allowable resistance to airflow. In general, cyclone collectors are often used to control industrial dust emissions and as pre-cleaners for other kinds of collection devices. Wet scrubbers are usually applied in the control of flammable or explosive dusts or mists from such sources as industrial and chemical processing facilities and hazardous-waste incinerators; they can handle hot airstreams and sticky particles. Electrostatic precipitators and fabric-filter baghouses are often used at power plants.

CYCLONES

A cyclone removes particulates by causing the dirty airstream to flow in a spiral path inside a cylindrical chamber. Dirty air enters the chamber from a tangential direction at the outer wall of the device, forming a vortex as it swirls within the chamber. The larger particulates, because of their greater inertia, move outward and are forced against the chamber wall. Slowed by friction with the wall surface, they then slide down the wall into a conical dust hopper at the bottom of the cyclone. The cleaned air swirls upward in a narrower spiral through an inner cylinder and emerges from an outlet at the top. Accumulated particulate dust is periodically removed from the hopper for disposal.

Cyclones are best at removing relatively coarse particulates. They can routinely achieve efficiencies of 90 percent for particles larger than about 20 micrometres (μm; 20 millionths of a metre). By themselves, however, cyclones are not sufficient to meet stringent air quality standards. They are typically used as pre-cleaners and are followed by more efficient air-cleaning equipment such as electrostatic precipitators and baghouses (described below).

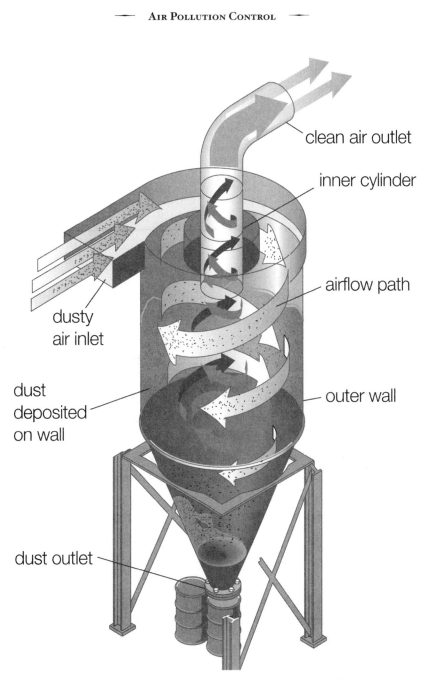

clean air outlet

inner cylinder

airflow path

outer wall

dusty air inlet

dust deposited on wall

dust outlet

Cyclone collector, for removing relatively coarse particulates from the air. Small cyclone devices are often installed to control pollution from mobile sources. Encyclopædia Britannica, Inc.

SCRUBBERS

Devices called wet scrubbers trap suspended particles by direct contact with a spray of water or other liquid. In effect, a scrubber washes the particulates out of the dirty airstream as they collide with and are entrained by the countless tiny droplets in the spray.

Several configurations of wet scrubbers are in use. In a spray-tower scrubber, an upward-flowing airstream is washed by water sprayed downward from a series of nozzles. The water is recirculated after it is sufficiently cleaned to prevent clogging of the nozzles. Spray-tower scrubbers can remove 90 percent of particulates larger than about 8 μm.

In orifice scrubbers and wet-impingement scrubbers, the air-and-droplet mixture collides with a solid surface. Collision with a surface atomizes the droplets, reducing droplet size and thereby increasing total surface contact area. These devices have the advantage of lower water-recirculation rates, and they offer removal efficiencies of about 90 percent for particles larger than 2 μm.

Venturi scrubbers are the most efficient of the wet collectors, achieving efficiencies of more than 98 percent for particles larger than 0.5 μm in diameter. Scrubber efficiency depends on the relative velocity between the droplets and the particulates. Venturi scrubbers achieve high relative velocities by injecting water into the throat of a venturi channel—a constriction in the flow path—through which particulate-laden air is passing at high speed.

ELECTROSTATIC PRECIPITATORS

Electrostatic precipitation is a commonly used method for removing fine particulates from airstreams. In an electrostatic precipitator, particles suspended in the airstream are given an electric charge as they enter the unit and are then removed by the influence of an electric field. The precipitation unit comprises baffles for distributing airflow, discharge and collection electrodes, a dust clean-out system, and collection hoppers. A high voltage of direct current (DC), as much as 100,000 volts, is applied to the discharge electrodes to charge the particles, which then are attracted to oppositely charged collection electrodes, on which they become trapped.

In a typical unit the collection electrodes comprise a group of large rectangular metal plates suspended vertically and parallel to each other inside a boxlike structure. There are often hundreds of plates having a combined surface area of tens of thousands of square metres. Rows of discharge electrode wires hang between the collection plates. The wires are given a negative electric charge, whereas the plates are grounded and thus become positively charged.

Particles that stick to the collection plates are removed periodically when the plates are shaken, or "rapped." Rapping is a mechanical technique for separating the trapped particles from the plates, which typically become covered with a 6-mm (0.2-inch) layer of dust. Rappers are either of the impulse (single-blow) or vibrating type. The dislodged particles are collected in a hopper at the bottom of the unit and removed for disposal. An electrostatic precipitator can remove particulates as small as 1 μm with an efficiency exceeding 99 percent. The effectiveness of electrostatic precipitators in removing fly ash from the combustion gases of fossil-fuel furnaces accounts for their high frequency of use at power stations.

BAGHOUSE FILTERS

One of the most efficient devices for removing suspended particulates is an assembly of fabric filter bags, commonly

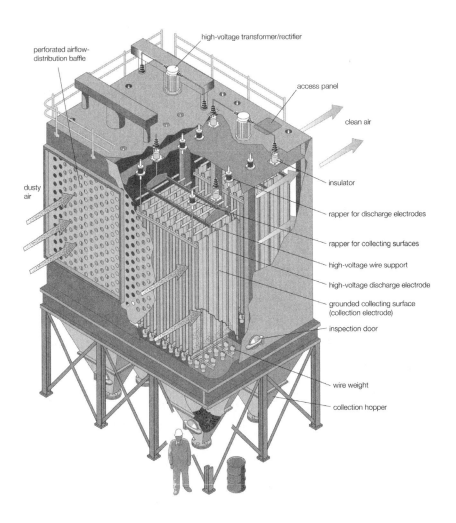

Electrostatic precipitator, a common particle-collection device at fossil-fuel power-generating stations. Encyclopædia Britannica, Inc.

called a baghouse. A typical baghouse comprises an array of long, narrow bags—each about 25 cm (10 inches) in diameter—that are suspended upside down in a large enclosure. Dust-laden air is blown upward through the bottom of the enclosure by fans. Particulates are trapped inside the filter bags, while the clean air passes through the fabric and exits at the top of the baghouse.

A fabric-filter dust collector can remove very nearly 100 percent of particles as small as 1 μm and a significant fraction of particles as small as 0.01 μm. Fabric filters,

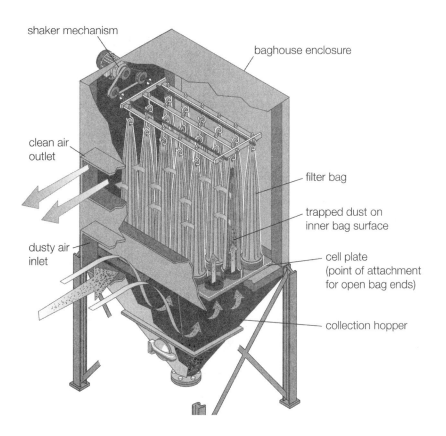

Baghouse employing an array of fabric bags for filtering the airstream. Encyclopædia Britannica, Inc.

however, offer relatively high resistance to airflow, and they are expensive to operate and maintain. In addition, in order to prolong the useful life of the filter fabric, the air to be cleaned must be cooled (usually below 300 °C [570 °F]) before it is passed through the unit; cooling coils needed for this purpose add to the expense. (Certain filter fabrics—e.g., those made of ceramic or mineral materials—can operate at higher temperatures.)

Several compartments of filter bags are often used at a single baghouse installation. This arrangement allows individual compartments to be cleaned while others remain in service. The bags are cleaned by mechanical shakers or by reversing the flow of air, and the loosened particulates are collected and removed for disposal.

CONTROL OF GASES

Gaseous criteria pollutants, as well as volatile organic compounds (VOCs) and other gaseous air toxics, are controlled by means of three basic techniques: absorption, adsorption, and incineration (or combustion). These techniques can be employed singly or in combination. They are effective against the major greenhouse gases as well. In addition, a fourth technique, known as carbon sequestration, is in development as a means of controlling carbon dioxide levels.

ABSORPTION

In the context of air pollution control, absorption involves the transfer of a gaseous pollutant from the air into a contacting liquid, such as water. The liquid must be able either to serve as a solvent for the pollutant or to capture it by means of a chemical reaction.

WET SCRUBBERS AND PACKED SCRUBBERS

Wet scrubbers similar to those described above for controlling suspended particulates may be used for gas absorption. Gas absorption can also be carried out in packed scrubbers, or towers, in which the liquid is present on a wetted surface rather than as droplets suspended in the air. A common type of packed scrubber is the countercurrent tower. After entering the bottom of the tower, the polluted airstream flows upward through a wetted column of light, chemically inactive packing material. The liquid absorbent flows downward and is uniformly spread throughout the column packing, thereby increasing the total area of contact between gas and liquid. Thermoplastic materials are most widely used as packing for countercurrent scrubber towers. These devices usually have gas-removal efficiencies of 90–95 percent.

Cocurrent and cross-flow packed scrubber designs are also used for gas absorption. In the cocurrent design, both gas and liquid flow in the same direction—vertically downward through the scrubber. Although not as efficient as countercurrent designs, cocurrent devices can work at higher liquid flow rates. The increased flow prevents plugging of the packing when the airstream contains high levels of particulates. Cocurrent designs afford lowered resistance to airflow and allow the cross-sectional area of the tower to be reduced. The cross-flow design, in which gas flows horizontally through the packing and liquid flows vertically downward, can operate with lower airflow resistance when high particulate levels are present.

In general, scrubbers are used at fertilizer production facilities (to remove ammonia from the airstream), at glass production plants (to remove hydrogen fluoride), at chemical plants (to remove water-soluble solvents such as acetone and methyl alcohol), and at rendering plants (to control odours).

Flue Gas Desulfurization

Sulfur dioxide in flue gas from fossil-fuel power plants can be controlled by means of an absorption process called flue gas desulfurization (FGD). FGD systems may involve wet scrubbing or dry scrubbing. In wet FGD systems, flue gases are brought in contact with an absorbent, which can be either a liquid or a slurry of solid material. The sulfur dioxide dissolves in or reacts with the absorbent and becomes trapped in it. In dry FGD systems, the absorbent is dry pulverized lime or limestone; once absorption occurs, the solid particles are removed by means of baghouse filters (described previously). Dry FGD systems, compared with wet systems, offer cost and energy savings and easier operation, but they require higher chemical consumption and are limited to flue gases derived from the combustion of low-sulfur coal.

FGD systems are also classified as either regenerable or nonregenerable (throwaway), depending on whether the sulfur that is removed from the flue gas is recovered or discarded. In the United States most systems in operation are nonregenerable because of their lower capital and operating costs. By contrast, in Japan regenerable systems are used extensively, and in Germany they are required by law. Nonregenerable FGD systems produce a sulfur-containing sludge residue that requires appropriate disposal. Regenerable FGD systems require additional steps to convert the sulfur dioxide into useful by-products like sulfuric acid.

Several FGD methods exist, differing mainly in the chemicals used in the process. FGD processes that employ either lime or limestone slurries as the reactants are widely

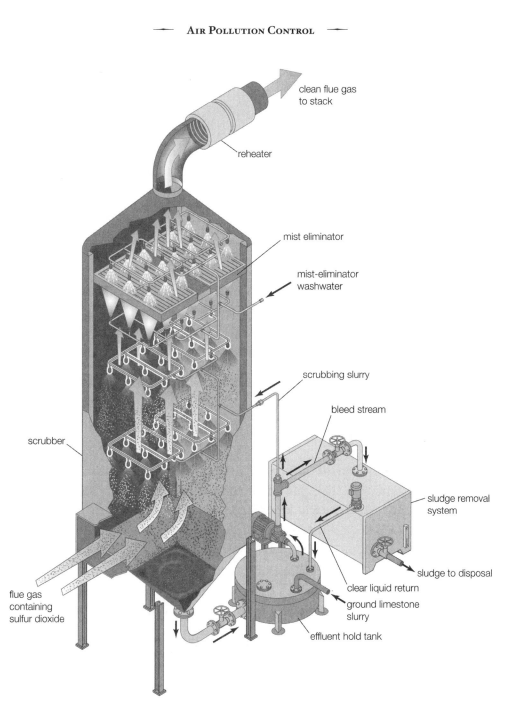

Wet scrubber using a limestone slurry to remove sulfur dioxide from flue gas.
Encyclopædia Britannica, Inc.

applied. In the limestone scrubbing process, sulfur dioxide reacts with limestone (calcium carbonate) particles in the slurry, forming calcium sulfite and carbon dioxide. In the lime scrubbing process, sulfur dioxide reacts with slaked lime (calcium hydroxide), forming calcium sulfite and water. Depending on sulfur dioxide concentrations and oxidation conditions, the calcium sulfite can continue to react with water, forming calcium sulfate (gypsum). Neither calcium sulfite nor calcium sulfate is very soluble in water, and both can be precipitated out as a slurry by gravity settling. The thick slurry, called FGD sludge, creates a significant disposal problem. Flue gas desulfurization helps to reduce ambient sulfur dioxide levels and mitigate the problem of acid rain. Nevertheless, in addition to its expense (which is passed on directly to the consumer as higher rates for electricity), millions of tons of FGD sludge are generated each year.

ADSORPTION

Gas adsorption, as contrasted with absorption, is a surface phenomenon. The gas molecules are sorbed—attracted to and held—on the surface of a solid. Gas adsorption methods are used for odour control at various types of chemical-manufacturing and food-processing facilities, in the recovery of a number of volatile solvents (e.g., benzene), and in the control of VOCs at industrial facilities.

Activated carbon (heated charcoal) is one of the most common adsorbent materials. It is very porous and has an extremely high ratio of surface area to volume. Activated carbon is particularly useful as an adsorbent for cleaning airstreams that contain VOCs and for solvent recovery and odour control. A properly designed carbon adsorption unit can remove gas with an efficiency exceeding 95 percent.

Adsorption systems are configured either as stationary bed units or as moving bed units. In stationary bed adsorbers, the polluted airstream enters from the top, passes through a layer, or bed, of activated carbon, and exits at the bottom. In moving bed adsorbers, the activated carbon moves slowly down through channels by gravity as the air to be cleaned passes through in a cross-flow current.

INCINERATION

The process called incineration or combustion—chemically, rapid oxidation—can be used to convert VOCs and other gaseous hydrocarbon pollutants to carbon dioxide and water. Incineration of VOCs and hydrocarbon fumes usually is accomplished in a special incinerator called an afterburner. To achieve complete combustion, the afterburner must provide the proper amount of turbulence and burning time, and it must maintain a sufficiently high temperature. Sufficient turbulence, or mixing, is a key factor in combustion because it reduces the required burning time and temperature. A process called direct flame incineration can be used when the waste gas is itself a combustible mixture and does not need the addition of air or fuel.

An afterburner typically is made of a steel shell lined with refractory material such as firebrick. The refractory lining protects the shell and serves as a thermal insulator. Given enough time and high enough temperatures, gaseous organic pollutants can be almost completely oxidized, with incineration efficiency approaching 100 percent. Certain substances, such as platinum, can act in a manner that assists the combustion reaction. These substances, called catalysts, allow complete oxidation of the combustible gases at relatively low temperatures.

Afterburners are used to control odours, destroy toxic compounds, or reduce the amount of photochemically reactive substances released into the air. They are employed at a variety of industrial facilities where VOC vapours are emitted from combustion processes or solvent evaporation (e.g., petroleum refineries, paint-drying facilities, and paper mills).

CARBON SEQUESTRATION

The best way to reduce the levels of carbon dioxide in the air is to use energy more efficiently and to reduce the combustion of fossil fuels by using alternative energy sources (e.g., nuclear, wind, tidal, and solar power). In addition, carbon sequestration can be used to serve the purpose. Carbon sequestration involves the long-term storage of carbon dioxide underground, as well as on the surface of Earth in forests and oceans. Carbon sequestration in forests and oceans relies on natural processes such as forest growth. However, the clearing of forests for agricultural and other purposes (and also the pollution of oceans) diminishes natural carbon sequestration. Storing carbon dioxide underground—a technology under development that is also called geosequestration or carbon capture and storage—would involve pumping the gas directly into underground geologic "reservoir" layers. This would require the separation of carbon dioxide from power plant flue gases (or some other source)—a costly process.

AUTOMOBILE EMISSION CONTROL SYSTEMS

By-products of the operation of the gasoline engine include carbon monoxide, oxides of nitrogen, and hydrocarbons (unburned fuel compounds), each of which is a pollutant.

To control the air pollution resulting from these emissions, governments establish quality standards and perform inspections to ensure that standards are met. Standards have become progressively more stringent, and the equipment necessary to meet them has become more complex.

To alter the characteristics of emissions, various engine modifications have been successfully introduced. These include adjusted air-fuel ratios, lowered compression ratios, retarded spark timing, reduced combustion chamber surface-to-volume ratios, and closer production tolerances. To improve drivability ("responsiveness") of some arrangements, preheated air from a heat exchanger on the exhaust manifold is ducted to the air cleaner.

In addition to such measures intended to improve the operation of the gasoline engine, various technologies are employed to limit the emission of noxious gases at their source. There are three main sources of these gases: the engine exhaust, the crankcase, and the fuel tank and carburetor. The exhaust pipe discharges burned and unburned hydrocarbons, carbon monoxide, oxides of nitrogen and sulfur, and traces of various acids, alcohols, and phenols. The crankcase is a secondary source of unburned hydrocarbons and, to a lesser extent, carbon monoxide. In the fuel tank and (in older automobiles) the carburetor, hydrocarbons that are continually evaporating from gasoline constitute a minor but not insignificant contributing factor in pollution. A variety of systems for controlling emissions from all these sources have been developed.

In the crankcase—the portion of the engine block below the cylinders where the crankshaft is located—leaked combustion gases are combined with ventilating air and returned to the intake manifold for reburning in the combustion chamber. The device that performs this function is known as the positive crankcase ventilation valve, or PCV valve.

To control exhaust emissions, which are responsible for two-thirds of the total engine pollutants, two types of systems are used: the air-injection system and the exhaust gas recirculation (EGR) system. In EGR a certain portion of exhaust gases are directed back to the cylinder head, where they are combined with the fuel-air mixture and enter the combustion chamber. The recirculated exhaust gases serve to lower the temperature of combustion, a condition that favours lower production of nitrogen oxides as combustion products (though at some loss of engine efficiency). In a typical air-injection system, an engine-driven pump injects air into the exhaust manifold, where the air combines with unburned hydrocarbons and carbon monoxide at a high temperature and, in effect, continues the combustion process. In this way a large percentage of the pollutants that were formerly discharged through the exhaust system are burned (though with no additional generation of power).

Another area for additional combustion is the catalytic converter, consisting of an insulated chamber containing ceramic pellets or a ceramic honeycomb structure coated with a thin layer of metals such as platinum and palladium. As the exhaust gases are passed through the packed beads or the honeycomb, the metals act as catalysts to induce the hydrocarbons, carbon monoxide, and nitrogen oxides in the exhaust to convert to water vapour, carbon dioxide, and nitrogen. These systems are not completely effective: during warm-up the temperatures are so low that emissions cannot be catalyzed. Preheating the catalytic converter is a possible solution to this problem; the high-voltage batteries in hybrid cars, for example, can provide enough power to heat up the converter very quickly.

In the past, gasoline fumes evaporating from the fuel tank and carburetor were vented directly into the atmosphere. Today those emissions are greatly reduced by sealed fuel-tank caps and the so-called evaporative control system, the heart of which is a canister of activated charcoal capable of holding up to 35 percent of its own weight in fuel vapour. In operation, fuel-tank vapours flow from the sealed fuel tank to a vapour separator, which returns raw fuel to the tank and channels fuel vapour through a purge valve to the canister. The canister acts as a storehouse; when the engine is running, the vapours are drawn by the resultant vacuum from the canister, through a filter, and into the combustion chamber, where they are burned.

Improvements in combustion efficiency are effected by computerized control over the whole process of combustion. This control ensures the most efficient operation of the systems described above. In addition, computer-controlled fuel-injection, as a replacement for carburetion, is widely employed to reduce exhaust emissions. The precise metering of fuel for each cylinder provides a means of ensuring that the chemically correct air-to-fuel ratio is being burned in the engine. This eliminates cylinder-to-cylinder variations and the tendency of cylinders that are most remote from the carburetor to receive less fuel than is desired. A variety of metering and control systems are commercially available. Timed injection, in which a small quantity of gasoline is squirted into each cylinder or intake-valve port during the intake stroke of the piston, is employed on a number of cars. Such systems ensure greater efficiency in combustion and lower generation of pollutants.

CHAPTER 4
POLLUTION ON LAND

A ll around the world solid or liquid waste materials are deposited on land or underground in a manner that can contaminate the soil and groundwater, threaten public health, and cause unsightly conditions and nuisances. The waste materials that cause land pollution are broadly classified as municipal solid waste (MSW, also called municipal refuse), construction and demolition (C&D) waste or debris, and hazardous waste. MSW includes nonhazardous garbage, rubbish, and trash from homes, institutions (e.g., schools), commercial establishments, and industrial facilities. C&D waste (or debris) includes wood and metal objects, wallboard, concrete rubble, asphalt, and other inert materials produced when structures are built, renovated, or demolished. Hazardous wastes include harmful and dangerous substances generated primarily as liquids but also as solids, sludges, or gases by various chemical manufacturing companies, petroleum refineries, paper mills, smelters, machine shops, dry cleaners, automobile repair shops, and many other industries or commercial facilities.

In addition to improper disposal of MSW, C&D waste, and hazardous waste, contaminated effluent from subsurface sewage disposal (e.g., from septic tanks) can also be a cause of land pollution, as can the presence of nonbiological chemical compounds in soils.

SOLID WASTE

All nonhazardous solid waste from a community that requires collection and transport to a processing or disposal site is called refuse or municipal solid waste (MSW). Refuse includes garbage and rubbish. Garbage contains moist and decomposable (biodegradable) food wastes (e.g., meat and vegetable scraps), while rubbish comprises mostly dry materials such as paper, glass, textiles, and plastic objects. Trash is rubbish that includes bulky items such as old refrigerators, couches, or large tree stumps. Trash requires special collection and handling.

Construction and demolition (C&D) waste is a significant component of total solid waste quantities (about 20 percent in the United States), although it is not considered to be part of the MSW stream. However, because C&D waste is inert and nonhazardous, it is usually disposed of in municipal sanitary landfills (described below).

Another type of solid waste, perhaps the fastest-growing component in many developed countries, is electronic waste, or e-waste, which includes discarded computer equipment, televisions, telephones, and a variety of other electronic devices. In the United States, e-waste entering the MSW stream grew from 2.63 million tons in 2005 to 3.01 million tons in 2007—an increase of 14 percent in a time period when the total MSW stream in the United States grew by 1.5 percent. Concern over this type of waste is escalating. Lead, mercury, and cadmium are among the materials of concern in electronic devices, and governmental policies may be required to regulate their recycling and disposal.

Solid-waste characteristics vary considerably among communities and nations. American refuse is usually lighter, for example, than European or Japanese refuse. In the United States paper and paperboard products make up close to 40 percent of the total weight of MSW; food waste accounts for less than 10 percent. The rest is a mixture of yard trimmings, wood, glass, metal, plastic, leather, cloth, and other miscellaneous materials. In a loose or uncompacted state, MSW of this type weighs approximately 120 kg per cubic metre (200 pounds per cubic

Discarded electronics waiting to be recycled area on Hitaddu Island, Maldives. Toxic materials from old computers, televisions, and the like are a growing threat around the world. EyesWideOpen/Getty Images

yard). These figures vary with geographic location, economic conditions, season of the year, and many other factors. Waste characteristics from each community must be studied carefully before any treatment or disposal facility is designed and built.

Rates of solid-waste generation vary widely. In the United States, for example, municipal refuse is generated at an average rate of approximately 2 kg (4.4 pounds) per person per day. Japan generates roughly half this amount, yet in Canada the rate is 3 kg (almost 7 pounds) per person per day. In some developing countries (e.g., India) the average rate can be lower than 0.5 kilograms (1 pound) per person per day. These data include refuse from commercial, institutional, and industrial as well as residential sources. The actual rates of refuse generation must be carefully determined when a community plans a solid-waste management project.

HAZARDOUS WASTE

Certain types of wastes that cause immediate danger to exposed individuals or environments are classified as hazardous. Hazardous wastes are categorized on the basis of their biological, chemical, and physical properties. These properties generate materials that are either toxic, reactive, ignitable, corrosive, infectious, or radioactive.

Toxic wastes are poisons, even in very small or trace amounts. They may have acute effects, causing death or violent illness, or they may have chronic effects, slowly causing irreparable harm. Some are carcinogenic, causing cancer after many years of exposure. Others are mutagenic, causing major biological changes in the offspring of exposed humans and wildlife.

Reactive wastes are chemically unstable and react violently with air or water. They cause explosions or form toxic vapours. Ignitable wastes burn at relatively low temperatures and may cause an immediate fire hazard. Corrosive wastes include strong acidic or alkaline substances. They destroy solid material and living tissue upon contact, by chemical reaction.

Infectious wastes include used bandages, hypodermic needles, and other materials from hospitals or biological research facilities. Radioactive wastes emit ionizing energy that can harm living organisms. Because some radioactive materials can persist in the environment for many thousands of years before fully decaying, there is much concern over the control of these wastes. However, the handling and disposal of radioactive material is not a responsibility of local municipal government. Because of the scope and complexity of the problem, the management of radioactive waste—particularly nuclear fission waste—is usually considered an engineering task separate from other forms of hazardous-waste management.

MAJOR SOIL POLLUTANTS

	ROUTE TO ENVIRONMENT
Metals	
antimony (Sb)	metal products, paint, ceramics, rubber
beryllium (Be)	metal alloys
cadmium (Cd	galvanized metals, rubber, fungicides
chromium (Cr)	metal alloys, paint
copper (Cu)	metal products, pesticides
lead (Pb)	automobile parts, batteries, paint, fuel
mercury (Hg)	chlor-alkali products, electrical equipment, pesticides
nickel (Ni)	metal alloys, batteries
selenium (Se)	electronic products, glass, paint, plastics
silver (Ag)	metal alloys, photographic products
thallium (Tl)	metal alloys, electronic products
zinc (Zn)	galvanized metals, automobile parts, paint
Industrial wastes	
chlorinated solvents	industrial cleaning and degreasing activities
dioxins	waste incineration
lubricant additives	industrial and commercial operations
petroleum products	industrial and commercial operations
plasticizers	plastics manufacturing
polychlorinated biphenyls	electrical and chemical manufacturing

Pesticides	
aliphatic acids	herbicides
amides	herbicides
benzoics	herbicides
carbamates	herbicides
dinitroanilines	herbicides
dipyridyl	herbicides
phenoxyalkyl acids	herbicides
phenylureas	herbicides
triazines	herbicides
arsenicals	insecticides
carbamates	insecticides
chlorinated hydrocarbons	insecticides
organophosphates	insecticides
pyrethrum	insecticides
copper sulfate	fungicides
mercurials	fungicides
thiocarbamates	fungicides

XENOBIOTIC CHEMICALS IN SOIL

The presence of substances in soil that are not naturally produced by biological species is of great public concern. Many of these so-called xenobiotic (from Greek *xenos*, "stranger," and *bios*, "life") chemicals have been found to be carcinogens or may accumulate in the environment with toxic effects on ecosystems (see the table of major soil pollutants). Although human exposure to these substances is primarily through inhalation or drinking water, soils play an important role because they affect the mobility and biological impact of these toxins.

The abundance of xenobiotic compounds in soil has been increased dramatically by the accelerated rate of extraction of minerals and fossil fuels and by highly technological industrial processes. Most of the metals were typically found at very low total concentrations in pristine waters — for this reason they often are referred to as trace metals. Rapid increases of trace metal concentrations in the environment are commonly coupled to the development of exploitative technologies. This kind of sudden change exposes the biosphere to a risk of destabilization, since organisms that developed under conditions with low concentrations of a metal present have not developed biochemical pathways capable of detoxifying that metal when it is present at high concentrations. The same line of reasoning applies to the organic toxic compounds.

Not all soil pollutants are xenobiotic compounds. Crop production problems in agriculture are encountered when excess salinity (salt accumulation) occurs in soils in arid climates where the rate of evaporation exceeds the rate of precipitation. As the soil dries, ions released by mineral weathering or introduced by saline groundwater tend to accumulate in the form of carbonate, sulfate, chloride, and clay minerals. Because all sodium and potassium and many calcium and magnesium salts of chloride, sulfide, and carbonate are readily soluble, it is this set of metal ions that contributes most to soil salinity. At sufficiently high concentrations, the salts pose a toxicity hazard from sodium, bicarbonate, and chloride and interfere with water uptake by plants from soil. Toxicity from boron is also common because of the accumulation of boron-containing minerals in arid soil environments.

The sustained use of a water resource for irrigating agricultural land in an arid region requires that the applied water not damage the soil environment. Irrigation waters are also salt solutions; depending on their particular source

Farmers working on the tubes of an irrigation system in China. Such systems need to be monitored to ensure that salts and other chemical compounds in irrigation water will not harm the soil. ChinaFotoPress/Getty Images

and postwithdrawal treatment, the particular salts present in irrigation water may not be compatible with the suite of minerals present in the soils. Crop utilization of water and fertilizers has the effect of concentrating salts in the soil. Consequently, without careful management, irrigated soils can become saline or develop toxicity. A widespread example of irrigation-induced toxicity hazard is nitrate accumulation in groundwater caused by the excess leaching of nitrogen fertilizer through agricultural soil. Human infants receiving high-nitrate groundwater as drinking water can contract methemoglobinemia ("blue baby syndrome") because of the transformation of nitrate to toxic nitrite in the digestive tract. Costly groundwater treatment is currently the only remedy possible when this problem arises.

CHAPTER 5
WASTE MANAGEMENT AND SOIL DETOXIFICATION

Improper disposal of municipal solid waste can create unsanitary conditions, and these conditions in turn can lead to pollution of the environment and to outbreaks of vector-borne disease—that is, diseases spread by rodents and insects. For this reason, an important municipal service is solid-waste management—the collecting, treating, and disposing of solid material that is discarded because it has served its purpose or is no longer useful. The tasks of solid-waste management present complex technical challenges. They also pose a wide variety of administrative, economic, and social problems that must be managed and solved.

The disposal of hazardous waste also requires special attention because hazardous wastes can cause serious illnesses or injuries and can pose immediate and significant threats to environmental quality. Natural pathways of detoxification in soils, meanwhile, provide a demonstration of how nature's self-corrective mechanisms can be used to remediate a polluted environment.

DEVELOPMENTS IN WASTE MANAGEMENT

In ancient cities, wastes were thrown onto unpaved streets and roadways, where they were left to accumulate. It was not until 320 BCE in Athens that the first known law forbidding this practice was established. At that time a system for waste removal began to evolve in Greece and the Greek-dominated cities of the eastern Mediterranean. In ancient Rome, property owners were responsible for cleaning the streets fronting their property. But organized waste collection was associated only with state-sponsored events such as parades. Disposal methods were very crude, involving open pits located just outside the city walls. As populations increased, efforts were made to transport waste farther out from the cities.

After the fall of Rome, waste collection and municipal sanitation began a decline that lasted throughout the Middle Ages. Near the end of the 14th century, scavengers were given the task of carting waste to dumps outside city walls. But this was not the case in smaller towns, where most people still threw waste into the streets. It was not until 1714 that every city in England was required to have an official scavenger. Toward the end of the 18th century in America, municipal collection of garbage was begun in Boston, New York City, and Philadelphia. Waste disposal methods were still very crude, however. Garbage collected in Philadelphia, for example, was simply dumped into the Delaware River downstream from the city.

A technological approach to solid-waste management began to develop in the latter part of the 19th century. Watertight garbage cans were first introduced in the United States, and sturdier vehicles were used to collect and transport wastes. A significant development in solid-waste treatment and disposal practices was marked by the construction of the first refuse incinerator in England in 1874. By the beginning of the 20th century, 15 percent of major American cities were incinerating solid waste.

Technological advances continued during the first half of the 20th century, including the development of garbage grinders, compaction trucks, and pneumatic collection systems. Even then, however, solid wastes were generally collected and placed on top of the ground in uncontrolled "open dumps," which often became breeding grounds for rats, mosquitoes, flies, and other disease carriers and were sources of unpleasant odours, windblown debris, and other nuisances. Dumps can contaminate groundwater as well as pollute nearby streams and lakes. A highly contaminated liquid called leachate is generated from decomposition of garbage and precipitation that infiltrates and percolates downward through the volume of waste material. When leachate reaches and mixes with groundwater or seeps into nearby bodies of surface water, public health and environmental quality are jeopardized. Methane, a poisonous and explosive gas that easily flows through soil, is an eventual by-product of the anaerobic (in the absence of oxygen) decomposition of putrescible solid waste material.

By the middle of the 20th century it had become evident that open dumping and improper incineration of solid waste were causing problems of pollution and jeopardizing public health. As a result, sanitary landfills were developed to replace the practice of open dumping and to reduce the reliance on waste incineration. In many countries waste was divided into two categories, hazardous and nonhazardous, and separate regulations were developed for their disposal. Landfills were designed and operated in a manner that minimized risks to public health and the environment. New refuse incinerators were designed to recover heat energy from the waste and were provided with extensive air pollution control devices to satisfy stringent standards of air quality. Modern solid-waste management plants in most developed countries now emphasize the practice of recycling and waste reduction at the source rather than incineration and land disposal. Open dumping of solid waste is no longer allowed in many countries. Nevertheless, leachate and methane from old dumps continue to cause land pollution problems in some areas.

Before modern techniques for disposing of hazardous wastes were legislated and put into practice, the wastes were generally disposed of or stored in surface piles, lagoons, ponds, or unlined landfills. Thousands of those waste sites still exist, now old and abandoned. Also, the illegal but frequent practice of "midnight dumping" of hazardous wastes, as well as accidental spills, have contaminated thousands of industrial land parcels and continue to pose serious threats to public health and environmental quality. Efforts to remediate or clean up such sites will continue for years to come. In 1980 the United States Congress created the Superfund program and authorized billions of dollars toward site remediation; today there are still about 1,300 sites on the Superfund list requiring remediation. The first listed Superfund site—Love Canal, located in Niagara Falls, N.Y.—was not removed from the list until 2004.

STORAGE, COLLECTION, AND TRANSPORT

Most communities require household refuse to be stored in durable, easily cleaned containers with tight-fitting covers in order to minimize rodent or insect infestation and offensive odours. Galvanized metal or plastic containers of about 115-litre (30-gallon) capacity are commonly used, although some communities employ larger containers that can be mechanically lifted and emptied into collection trucks. Plastic bags are frequently used as liners or as disposable containers for curbside collection. Where large quantities of refuse are generated—such as at shopping centres, hotels, or apartment buildings—dumpsters may be used for temporary storage until the waste is collected. Some office and commercial buildings use on-site compactors to reduce the waste volume.

Proper solid-waste collection is important for the protection of public health, safety, and environmental quality. It is a labour-intensive activity, accounting for approximately three-quarters of the total cost of solid-waste management. Public employees are often assigned to the task, but sometimes it is more economical for private companies to do the work under contract to the municipality or for private collectors to be paid by individual home owners. A driver and one or two loaders serve each collection vehicle. These are typically trucks of the enclosed, compacting type, with capacities up to 30 cubic metres (40 cubic yards). Loading can be done from the front, rear, or side. Compaction reduces the volume of refuse in the truck to less than half of its loose volume.

The task of selecting an optimal collection route is a complex problem, especially for large and densely populated cities. An optimal route is one that results in the most efficient use of labour and equipment, and selecting such a route requires the application of computer analyses that account for all the many design variables in a large and complex network. Variables include frequency of collection, haulage distance, type of service, and climate. Collection of refuse in rural areas can present a special problem, since the population densities are low, leading to high unit costs.

Refuse collection usually occurs at least once per week because of the rapid decomposition of food waste. The amount of garbage in the refuse of an individual home can be reduced by garbage grinders, or garbage disposals. Ground garbage puts an extra load on sewerage systems, but this can usually be accommodated. Many communities now conduct source separation and recycling programs, in which homeowners and businesses separate recyclable materials from garbage and place them in separate containers for collection. In addition, some communities have drop-off centres where residents can bring recyclables.

If the final destination of the refuse is not near the community in which it is generated, one or more transfer stations may be necessary. A transfer station is a central facility where refuse from many collection vehicles is combined into a larger vehicle, such as a tractor-trailer unit. Open-top trailers are designed to carry about 76 cubic metres (100 cubic yards) of uncompacted waste to a regional processing or disposal location. Closed compactor-type trailers are also available, but they must be equipped with ejector mechanisms. In a direct discharge type of station, several collection trucks empty directly into the transport vehicle. In a storage discharge type of station, refuse is first emptied into a storage pit or onto a platform, and then machinery is used to hoist or push the solid waste into the transport vehicle. Large transfer stations can handle more than 500 tons of refuse per day.

SOLID-WASTE TREATMENT AND DISPOSAL

Once collected, municipal solid waste may be treated in order to reduce the total volume and weight of material that requires final disposal. Treatment changes the form of the waste and makes it easier to handle. It can also serve to recover certain materials, as well as heat energy, for recycling or reuse.

INCINERATION

Burning is a very effective method of reducing the volume and weight of solid waste. In modern incinerators the waste is burned inside a properly designed furnace under very carefully controlled conditions. The combustible portion of the waste combines with oxygen, releasing mostly carbon dioxide, water vapour, and heat. Incineration can reduce the volume of uncompacted waste by more than 90 percent, leaving an inert residue of ash, glass, metal, and other solid materials called bottom ash. The gaseous by-products of incomplete combustion, along with finely divided particulate material called fly ash, are carried along in the incinerator airstream. Fly ash includes cinders, dust, and soot. In order to remove fly ash and gaseous by-products before they are exhausted into the atmosphere, modern incinerators must be equipped with extensive emission control devices. Such devices include fabric baghouse filters, acid gas scrubbers, and electrostatic precipitators. Bottom ash and fly ash are usually combined and disposed of in a landfill. If the ash is found to contain toxic metals, it must be managed as a hazardous waste.

Municipal solid-waste incinerators are designed to receive and burn a continuous supply of refuse. A deep refuse storage pit, or tipping area, provides enough space for about one day of waste storage. The refuse is lifted from the pit by a crane equipped with a bucket or grapple

A soldier stands in front of a newly opened incinerator in Italy. AFP/ Getty Images

device. It is then deposited into a hopper and chute above the furnace and released onto a charging grate or stoker. The grate shakes and moves waste through the furnace, allowing air to circulate around the burning material. Modern incinerators are usually built with a rectangular furnace, although rotary kiln furnaces and vertical circular furnaces are available. Furnaces are constructed of refractory bricks that can withstand the high combustion temperatures.

Combustion in a furnace occurs in two stages: primary and secondary. In primary combustion, moisture is driven off, and the waste is ignited and volatilized. In secondary combustion, the remaining unburned gases and particulates are oxidized, eliminating odours and reducing the amount of fly ash in the exhaust. When the refuse is very moist, auxiliary gas or fuel oil is sometimes burned to start the primary combustion.

In order to provide enough oxygen for both primary and secondary combustion, air must be thoroughly mixed with the burning refuse. Air is supplied from openings beneath the grates or is admitted to the area above. The relative amounts of this underfire air and overfire air must be determined by the plant operator to achieve good combustion efficiency. A continuous flow of air can be maintained by a natural draft in a tall chimney or by mechanical forced-draft fans.

COMPOSTING

Another method of treating municipal solid waste is composting, a biological process in which the organic portion of refuse is allowed to decompose under carefully controlled conditions. Microbes metabolize the organic waste material and reduce its volume by as much as 50 percent. The stabilized product is called compost or humus. It

WASTE TO ENERGY

The energy value of incinerated refuse can be as much as one-third that of coal, depending on the paper content, and the heat given off during incineration can be recovered by the use of a refractory-lined furnace coupled to a boiler. Boilers convert the heat of combustion into steam or hot water, thus allowing the energy content of the refuse to be recycled. Incinerators that recycle heat energy in this way are called waste-to-energy plants. Instead of a separate furnace and boiler, a water-tube wall furnace may also be used for energy recovery. Such a furnace is lined with vertical steel tubes spaced closely enough to form continuous sections of wall. The walls are insulated on the outside in order to reduce heat loss. Water circulating through the tubes absorbs heat to produce steam, and it also helps to control combustion temperatures without the need for excessive air, thus lowering air-pollution control costs.

Waste-to-energy plants operate as either mass burn or refuse-derived fuel systems. A mass burn system uses all the refuse, without prior treatment or preparation. A refuse-derived fuel system separates combustible wastes from noncombustibles such as glass and metal before burning. If a turbine is installed at the plant, both steam and electricity can be produced in a process called cogeneration.

Waste-to-energy systems are more expensive to build and operate than plain incinerators because of the need for special equipment and controls, highly skilled technical personnel, and auxiliary fuel systems. On the other hand, the sale of generated steam or electricity offsets much of the extra cost, and recovery of heat energy from refuse is a viable solid-waste management option from both an engineering and an economic point of view. About 80 percent of municipal refuse incinerators in the United States are waste-to-energy facilities.

resembles potting soil in texture and odour and may be used as a soil conditioner or mulch.

Composting offers a method of processing and recycling both garbage and sewage sludge in one operation. As more stringent environmental rules and siting constraints limit the use of solid-waste incineration and landfill options, the application of composting is likely to increase. The steps involved in the process include sorting and separating, size reduction, and digestion of the refuse.

SORTING AND SHREDDING

The decomposable materials in refuse are isolated from glass, metal, and other inorganic items through sorting and separating operations. These are carried out mechanically, using differences in such physical characteristics of the refuse as size, density, and magnetic properties. Shredding or pulverizing reduces the size of the waste articles, resulting in a uniform mass of material. It is accomplished with hammer mills and rotary shredders.

DIGESTING AND PROCESSING

Pulverized waste is ready for composting either by the open windrow method or in an enclosed mechanical facility. Windrows are long, low mounds of refuse. They are turned or mixed every few days to provide air for the microbes digesting the organics. Depending on moisture conditions, it may take five to eight weeks for complete digestion of the waste. Because of the metabolic action of aerobic bacteria, temperatures in an active compost pile reach about 65 °C (150 °F), killing pathogenic organisms that may be in the waste material.

Open windrow composting requires relatively large land areas. Enclosed mechanical composting facilities can reduce land requirements by about 85 percent. Mechanical composting systems employ one or more closed tanks or digesters equipped with rotating vanes that mix and aerate the shredded waste. Complete digestion of the waste takes about one week.

Digested compost must be processed before it can be used as a mulch or soil conditioner. Processing includes drying, screening, and granulating or pelletizing. These steps improve the market value of the compost, which is the most serious constraint to the success of composting as a waste management option. Agricultural demand for digested compost is usually low because of the high cost of transporting it and because of competition with inorganic chemical fertilizers.

Windrow composting allows organic debris to ferment in the open air. Shutterstock.com

SANITARY LANDFILLS

A modern technique for land disposal of solid waste involves construction and daily operation and control of so-called sanitary landfills. Sanitary landfills are not dumps; they are carefully planned and engineered facilities designed to control leachate and methane and minimize the risk of land pollution from solid-waste disposal. Engineering design requirements include a minimum distance between the bottom of the landfill and the seasonally high groundwater table. Most new landfills are required to have an impermeable liner or barrier at the bottom, as well as a system of groundwater-monitoring wells. Completed landfill sections must be capped with an impermeable cover to keep precipitation or surface runoff away from the buried waste. Bottom and cap liners may be made of flexible plastic membranes, layers of clay soil, or a combination of both.

CONSTRUCTING THE LANDFILL

The basic element of a sanitary landfill is the refuse cell. This is a confined portion of the site in which refuse is spread and compacted in thin layers. Several layers may be compacted on top of one another to a maximum depth of about 3 metres (10 ft). The compacted refuse occupies about one-quarter of its original loose volume. At the end of each day's operation, the refuse is covered with a layer of soil to eliminate windblown litter, odours, and insect or rodent problems. One refuse cell thus contains the daily volume of compacted refuse and soil cover. Several adjacent refuse cells make up a lift, and eventually a landfill may comprise two or more lifts stacked one on top of the other. The final cap for a completed landfill may also be covered with a layer of topsoil that can support vegetative growth.

A poster delineating the many layers that make up a sanitary landfill in Ohio.
Careful planning and engineering differentiate sanitary landfills from dumps.
Courtesy of the Solid Waste Authority of Central Ohio (SWACO)

SWACO SANITARY LANDFILL

CLOSED VERTICAL CELLS
A cell that has reached full capacity as determined by the state environmental regulatory agency.

SCALE HOUSE
Weighs garbage trucks and other vehicles in order to determine the amount of garbage deposited in the landfill. The tipping fee is also paid at the scale house.

RADIATION MONITOR
A device that detects radioactive material.

TIPPER
An efficient machine used to tip and empty trailers filled with garbage.

RESIDENTIAL DROP-OFF
A separate area designated for residents to unload garbage.

COMPACTOR
A large machine with heavy steel wheels and spikes used to spread and compact garbage.

GROUNDWATER MONITORING WELLS

GEO-NET
Plastic webbing covered with filter fabric used to protect the leachate collection system.

REAR LOADER
One of the many types of trucks used to transport garbage to the landfill.

RE-COMPACTED CLAY LINER
3 feet of recompacted clay used to prevent soil and water contamination. A component of the side and bottom liner system.

GEO-SYNTHETIC CLAY LINER
180 mil bentonite mat used to prevent soil and water contamination. A component of the side and bottom liner system.

PLASTIC LINER
60 mil of HDPE used to prevent soil and water contamination. A component of the side and bottom liner system.

LEACHATE COLLECTION SYSTEM
Leachate or "Garbage Juice" is produced when rain water mixes with Household Hazardous Waste (HHW) deposited in the landfill. Permeable layers like sand, gravel and Geo-net allow leachate to pass through for collection while protecting the drainage system.

FILTER FABRIC
Woven mat used to help protect the leachate collection system.

93

Daily cover soil may be available on-site, or it may be hauled in and stockpiled from off-site sources. Various types of heavy machinery, such as crawler tractors or rubber-tired dozers, are used to spread and compact the refuse and soil. Heavy steel-wheeled compactors may also be employed to achieve high-density compaction of the refuse.

For a new landfill, the area and depth are carefully staked out, and the base is prepared for construction of any required liner and leachate-collection system. Where a plastic liner is used, at least 30 cm (12 inches) of sand is carefully spread over it to provide protection from landfill vehicles. At sites where excavations can be made below grade, the trench method of construction may be followed. Where this is not feasible because of topography or groundwater conditions, the area method may be practiced, resulting in a mound or hill rising above the original ground. Since no ground is excavated in the area method, soil usually must be hauled to the site from some other location. Variations of the area method may be employed where a landfill site is located on sloping ground, in a valley, or in a ravine. The completed landfill eventually blends in with the landscape.

The permeability of soil formations underlying a waste disposal site is of great importance with regard to land pollution. The greater the permeability, the greater the risks from land pollution. Soil consists of a mixture of unconsolidated mineral and rock fragments (gravel, sand, silt, and clay) formed from natural weathering processes. Gravel, sand, and silt are relatively coarse-grained bulky particles, while clay particles are very small and platelike in shape and have a strong affinity for water. Gravel and sand formations are porous and permeable, allowing the free flow of water through the pores or spaces between the particles. Silt is much less permeable than sand or gravel, because of its small particle and pore sizes, while clay is virtually impermeable to the flow of water, because of its platelike shape and molecular forces.

CONTROLLING BY-PRODUCTS

Organic material buried in a landfill decomposes by anaerobic microbial action. Complete decomposition usually takes more than 20 years. One of the by-products of this decomposition is methane gas. Methane is poisonous and explosive when diluted in the air, and it can flow long distances through porous layers of soil. If it is allowed to collect in basements or other confined areas, dangerous conditions may arise. In modern landfills, methane movement is controlled by impermeable barriers and by gas-venting systems. In some landfills the methane gas is collected and recovered for use as a fuel.

A highly contaminated liquid called leachate is another by-product of decomposition in sanitary landfills. Most leachate is the result of runoff that infiltrates the refuse cells and comes in contact with decomposing garbage. If leachate reaches the groundwater or seeps out onto the ground surface, serious environmental pollution problems can occur, including the possible contamination of drinking-water supplies. Methods of controlling leachate include the interception of surface water in order to prevent it from entering the landfill and the use of impermeable liners or barriers between the waste and the groundwater. New landfill sites should also be provided with groundwater-monitoring wells and leachate-collection and treatment systems.

IMPORTANCE IN WASTE MANAGEMENT

In communities where appropriate sites are available, sanitary landfills usually provide the most economical option for disposal of nonrecyclable refuse. However, it is becoming increasingly difficult to find sites that offer adequate capacity, accessibility, and environmental conditions.

Nevertheless, landfills will always play a key role in solid-waste management. It is not possible to recycle all components of solid waste, and there will always be residues from incineration and other treatment processes that will eventually require disposal underground. In addition, landfills can actually improve poor-quality land. In some communities properly completed landfills are converted into recreational parks, playgrounds, or golf courses.

HAZARDOUS-WASTE MANAGEMENT

Hazardous waste differs from MSW and C&D debris in both form and behaviour. The main characteristics of hazardous waste include toxicity, reactivity, ignitability, and corrosivity. In addition, waste products that may be infectious or are radioactive are also classified as hazardous waste. Although land disposal of hazardous waste is not always the best option, solid or containerized hazardous wastes can be disposed of by burial in "secure landfills," while liquid hazardous waste can be disposed of underground in deep-well injection systems if the geologic conditions are suitable. Some hazardous wastes such as dioxins, PCBs, cyanides, halogenated organics, and strong acids are banned from land disposal in the United States, unless they are first treated or stabilized or meet certain concentration limits.

Transport of Hazardous Waste

Hazardous waste generated at a particular site often requires transport to an approved treatment, storage, or disposal facility (TSDF). Because of potential threats to public safety and the environment, transport is given special attention by governmental agencies. In addition to the occasional accidental spill, hazardous waste has, in the past, been intentionally spilled or abandoned at random locations in a practice known as "midnight dumping." This practice has been greatly curtailed by the enactment of laws that require proper labeling, transport, and tracking of all hazardous wastes.

TRANSPORT VEHICLES

Hazardous waste is generally transported by truck over public highways. Only a very small amount is transported by rail, and almost none is moved by air or inland waterway. Highway shipment is the most common because road vehicles can gain access to most industrial sites and approved TSDFs. Railroad trains require expensive siding facilities and are suitable only for very large waste shipments.

Hazardous wastes can be shipped in tank trucks made of steel or aluminum alloy, with capacities up to about 34,000 litres (9,000 gallons). They also can be containerized and shipped in 200-litre (55-gallon) drums. Specifications and standards for cargo tank trucks and shipping containers are included in governmental regulations.

THE MANIFEST SYSTEM

In the United States a key feature of regulations pertaining to waste transport is the "cradle-to-grave" manifest system, which monitors the journey of hazardous waste from its point of origin to the point of final disposal. The manifest system helps to eliminate the problem of midnight dumping. It also provides a means for determining the type and quantity of hazardous waste being generated, as well as the recommended emergency procedures in case of an accidental spill. A manifest is a record-keeping document that must be prepared by the generator of the hazardous waste, such as a chemical manufacturer. The generator has primary responsibility for the ultimate disposal of the waste and must give the manifest, along with the waste itself, to a licensed waste transporter. A copy of the manifest must be delivered by the transporter to the recipient of the waste at an authorized TSDF. Each time the waste changes hands, a copy of the manifest must be signed. Copies of the manifest are kept by each party involved, and additional copies are sent to appropriate environmental agencies.

In the event of a leak or accidental spill of hazardous waste during its transport, the transporter must take immediate and appropriate actions, including notifying local authorities of the discharge. An area may have to be diked to contain the wastes, and efforts must be undertaken to remove the wastes and reduce environmental or public health hazards.

Treatment, Storage, and Disposal

Several options are available for hazardous-waste management. The most desirable is to reduce the quantity of waste at its source or to recycle the materials for some other productive use. Nevertheless, while reduction and recycling are desirable options, they are not regarded as the final remedy to the problem of hazardous-waste disposal. There will always be a need for treatment and storage or disposal of some amount of hazardous waste.

Treatment

Hazardous waste can be treated by chemical, thermal, biological, and physical methods. Chemical methods include ion exchange, precipitation, oxidation and reduction, and neutralization. Among thermal methods is high-temperature incineration, which not only can detoxify certain organic wastes but also can destroy them. Special types of thermal equipment are used for burning waste in either solid, liquid, or sludge form. These include the fluidized-bed incinerator, multiple-hearth furnace, rotary kiln, and liquid-injection incinerator. One problem posed by hazardous-waste incineration is the potential for air pollution.

Biological treatment of certain organic wastes, such as those from the petroleum industry, is also an option. One method used to treat hazardous waste biologically is called landfarming. In this technique the waste is carefully mixed with surface soil on a suitable tract of land. Microbes that can metabolize the waste may be added, along with nutrients. In some cases a genetically engineered species of bacteria is used. Food or forage crops are not grown on the same site. Microbes can also be used for stabilizing hazardous wastes on previously contaminated sites; in that case the process is called bioremediation.

The chemical, thermal, and biological treatment methods outlined above change the molecular form of the waste material. Physical treatment, on the other hand, concentrates, solidifies, or reduces the volume of the waste. Physical processes include evaporation, sedimentation, flotation, and filtration. Yet another process is solidification, which is achieved by encapsulating the waste in concrete, asphalt, or plastic. Encapsulation produces a solid mass of material that is resistant to leaching. Waste can also be mixed with lime, fly ash, and water to form a solid, cementlike product.

SURFACE STORAGE AND LAND DISPOSAL

Hazardous wastes that are not destroyed by incineration or other chemical processes need to be disposed of properly.

For most such wastes, land disposal is the ultimate destination, although it is not an attractive practice, because of the inherent environmental risks involved. Two basic methods of land disposal include landfilling and underground injection. Prior to land disposal, surface storage or containment systems are often employed as a temporary method.

Temporary on-site waste storage facilities include open waste piles and ponds or lagoons. New waste piles must be carefully constructed over an impervious base and must comply with regulatory requirements similar to those for landfills. The piles must be protected from wind dispersion or erosion. If leachate is generated, monitoring and control systems must be provided. Only noncontainerized solid, nonflowing waste material can be stored in a new waste pile, and the material must be landfilled when the size of the pile becomes unmanageable.

A common type of temporary storage impoundment for hazardous liquid waste is an open pit or holding pond, called a lagoon. New lagoons must be lined with impervious clay soils and flexible membrane liners in order to protect groundwater. Leachate collection systems must be installed between the liners, and groundwater monitoring wells are required. Except for some sedimentation, evaporation of volatile organics, and possibly some surface aeration, open lagoons provide no treatment of the waste. Accumulated sludge must be removed periodically and subjected to further handling as a hazardous waste.

Many older, unlined waste piles and lagoons are located above aquifers used for public water supply, thus posing significant risks to public health and environmental quality. A large number of these old sites have been identified and scheduled for cleanup, or remediation.

SECURE LANDFILLS

Landfilling of hazardous solid or containerized waste is regulated more stringently than landfilling of municipal solid waste. Hazardous wastes must be deposited in so-called secure landfills, which provide at least 3 metres (10 ft) of separation between the bottom of the landfill and the underlying bedrock or groundwater table. A secure hazardous-waste landfill must have two impermeable liners and leachate collection systems. The double leachate collection system consists of a network of perforated pipes placed above each liner. The upper system prevents the accumulation of leachate trapped in the fill, and the lower serves as a backup. Collected leachate is pumped to a treatment plant. In order to reduce the amount of leachate in the fill and minimize the potential for environmental damage, an impermeable cap or cover is placed over a finished landfill.

A groundwater monitoring system that includes a series of deep wells drilled in and around the site is also required. The wells allow a routine program of sampling and testing to detect any leaks or groundwater contamination. If a leak does occur, the wells can be pumped to intercept the polluted water and bring it to the surface for treatment.

One option for the disposal of liquid hazardous waste is deep-well injection, a procedure that involves pumping liquid waste through a steel casing into a porous layer of limestone or sandstone. High pressures are applied to force the liquid into the pores and fissures of the rock, where it is to be permanently stored. The injection zone must lie below a layer of impervious rock or clay, and it may extend more than 0.8 kilometres (0.5 miles) below the surface. Deep-well injection is relatively inexpensive and requires little or no pretreatment of the waste, but it poses a danger of leaking hazardous waste and eventually polluting subsurface water supplies.

LOVE CANAL

Love Canal was a neighbourhood in Niagara Falls, N.Y., that was the site of the worst environmental disaster involving chemical wastes in U.S. history.

The Love Canal area was originally the site of an abandoned canal that became a dumping ground for nearly 22,000 tons of chemical waste (including polychlorinated biphenyls, dioxin, and pesticides) produced by the Hooker Chemicals and Plastics Corporation in the 1940s and '50s. In the following years, the site was filled in and given by the company to the growing city of Niagara Falls, which allowed housing to be built on it. In 1978, however, state officials detected the leakage of toxic chemicals from underground into the basements of homes in the area.

Subsequent investigations established an abnormally high incidence of chromosomal damage among the area's residents, presumably caused by their long-term exposure to the toxic chemical wastes. Much of Love Canal was then evacuated, the abandoned land being purchased by the state of New York. The canal was capped and fenced off, and the buildings around it were razed. After protracted litigation, 1,300 former residents of Love Canal agreed to a $20 million settlement of their claims against the Occidental Chemical Corporation, which had taken over Hooker in the late 1960s, and the city of Niagara Falls.

In the early 1990s New York state ended its cleanup and declared parts of the Love Canal area safe to live in. The area north of the dump site was renamed Black Creek Village, and the state began to auction off houses there. In 1994 Occidental agreed to pay $98 million to New York to compensate the state for its contribution to the cleanup of Love Canal. The following year the company settled with the federal government as well, agreeing to pay $129 million over three years.

Remedial Action

Disposal of hazardous waste in unlined pits, ponds, or lagoons poses a threat to human health and environmental quality. Many such uncontrolled disposal sites were used in the past and have been abandoned. Depending on a determination of the level of risk, it may be necessary to remediate those sites. In some cases, the risk may require emergency action. In other instances, engineering studies may be required to assess the situation thoroughly before remedial action is undertaken.

One option for remediation is to completely remove all the waste material from the site and transport it to another location for treatment and proper disposal. This so-called off-site solution is usually the most expensive option. An alternative is on-site remediation, which reduces the production of leachate and lessens the chance of groundwater contamination. On-site remediation may include temporary removal of the hazardous waste, construction of a secure landfill on the same site, and proper replacement of the waste. It may also include treatment of any contaminated soil or groundwater. Treated soil may be replaced on-site and treated groundwater returned to the aquifer by deep-well injection.

A less costly alternative is full containment of the waste. This is done by placing an impermeable cover over the hazardous-waste site and by blocking the lateral flow of groundwater with subsurface cutoff walls. It is possible to use cutoff walls for this purpose when there is a natural layer of impervious soil or rock below the site. The walls are constructed around the perimeter of the site, deep enough to penetrate to the impervious layer. They can be excavated as trenches around the site without moving or disturbing the waste material. The trenches are filled with a bentonite clay slurry to prevent their collapse during construction, and they are backfilled with a mixture of soil and cement that solidifies to form an impermeable barrier. Cutoff walls thus serve as vertical barriers to the flow of water, and the impervious layer serves as a barrier at the bottom.

SOIL DETOXIFICATION

Field observation and laboratory experimentation have confirmed the effectiveness of natural pathways for detoxifying chemicals in soil. Various chemical transformations such as volatilization, adsorption, and precipitation, as well as biological immobilization and degradation, are the first line of defense against invasive pollutants. These processes are particularly active in the first metre (39 inches) of soil, where the reactivity of toxic chemicals is blocked by the finely divided organic matter known as humus or by microbial degradation.

Soil microorganisms, particularly bacteria, have developed diverse means to use readily available substances as sources of carbon or energy. Microorganisms obtain their energy by transferring electrons biochemically from organic matter (or from certain inorganic compounds) to electron acceptors such as oxygen and other inorganic compounds. Therefore, they provide a significant pathway for decomposing xenobiotic compounds in soil by using them as raw materials in place of naturally occurring organic matter or electron acceptors, such as oxygen, nitrate, manganese or iron ions, and sulfate.

For instance, one species of bacteria might use the pollutant toluene, a solvent obtained from petroleum, as a carbon source, and naturally occurring iron ions might serve as a normal electron acceptor. Another species might use natural organic acids as a carbon source and selenium-containing pollutants as electron acceptors. Often, however, the ultimate decomposition of a contaminating xenobiotic compound requires a series of many chemical steps and several different species of microorganism. This is especially true for organic compounds that contain chlorine, such as chlorinated pesticides, chlorinated solvents, and polychlorinated biphenyls (PCBs; once used as lubricants and plasticizers). For example, the chlorinated herbicide atrazine is gradually degraded by aerobic microorganisms through a variety of pathways involving intermediate products. The complexity of the decomposition processes and the inherent toxicity of the pollutant compounds to the microorganisms themselves can lead to long residence times in soil, ranging from years to decades for toxic metals and chlorinated organic compounds.

Most of the metals that are major soil pollutants can form strong complexes with soil humus that significantly decrease the solubility of the metal and its movement toward groundwater. Humus can serve as a detoxification pathway by assuming the role taken by biomolecules in the metal toxicity mechanisms discussed above. Just as strong complex formation leads to irreversible metal association with a biomolecule and to the disruption of biochemical functions, so, too, can it lead to effective immobilization of toxic metals by soil humus—in particular, the humic substances. The very property of toxic metals that makes them so hazardous to organisms also makes them detoxifiable by humus in soil.

Pesticides exhibit a wide variety of molecular structures that permit an equally diverse array of mechanisms of binding to humus. The diversity of molecular structures and reactivities results in the production of a variety of aromatic compounds through partial decomposition of the pesticides by microbes. These intermediate compounds become incorporated into the molecular structure of humus by natural mechanisms, effectively reducing the threat of toxicity. The benefits of humus to soil fertility and detoxification have resulted in a growing interest in this remarkable substance and in the fragile surface layer that it occupies.

RECYCLING

Recycling is the recovery and reprocessing of waste materials for use in new products. The basic phases in recycling are the collection of waste materials, their processing or manufacture into new products, and the purchase of those products, which may then themselves be recycled. Typical materials that are recycled include iron and steel scrap, aluminum cans, glass bottles, paper, wood, and plastics. The materials reused in recycling serve as substitutes for raw materials obtained from such increasingly scarce natural resources as petroleum, natural gas, coal, mineral ores, and trees. Recycling can help reduce the quantities of solid waste deposited in landfills, which have become increasingly expensive. Recycling also reduces the pollution not only of the land but also of the air and water resulting from waste disposal.

There are two broad types of recycling operations: internal and external. Internal recycling is the reuse in a manufacturing process of materials that are a waste product of that process. Internal recycling is common in the metals industry, for example. The manufacture of copper tubing results in a certain amount of waste in the form of tube ends and trimmings; this material is remelted and recast. Another form of internal recycling is seen in the distilling industry, in which, after the distillation, spent grain mash is dried and processed into an edible foodstuff for cattle.

External recycling is the reclaiming of materials from a product that has been worn out or rendered obsolete. An example of external recycling is the collection of old newspapers and magazines for repulping and their manufacture into new paper products. Aluminum cans and glass bottles are other examples of everyday objects that are externally recycled on a wide scale. These materials can be collected by any of three main methods: buy-back centres, which purchase waste materials that have been sorted and brought in by consumers; drop-off centres, where consumers can deposit waste materials but are not paid for them; and curbside collection, in which homes and businesses sort their waste materials and deposit them by the curb for collection by a central agency.

Society's choice of whether and how much to recycle depends basically on economic factors. Conditions of affluence and the presence of cheap raw materials encourage human beings' tendency to simply discard used

Plastic, glass, and metal containers in a recycling bin. © Brand X Pictures/
Jupiterimages Corporation

materials. Recycling becomes economically attractive when the cost of reprocessing waste or recycled material is less than the cost of treating and disposing of the materials or of processing new raw materials.

Separation

Before any material can be recycled, it must be separated from the raw waste and sorted. Separation can be accomplished at the source of the waste or at a central processing facility. Source separation, also called curbside separation, is done by individual citizens who collect newspapers, bottles, cans, and garbage separately and place them at the curb for collection. Many communities allow "commingling" of nonpaper recyclables (glass, metal, and plastic). In either case, municipal collection of source-separated refuse is more expensive than ordinary refuse collection.

In lieu of source separation, recyclable materials can be separated from garbage at centralized mechanical processing plants. Experience has shown that the quality of recyclables recovered from such facilities is lowered by contamination with moist garbage and broken glass. The best practice, as now recognized, is to have citizens separate refuse into a limited number of categories, including newspaper; magazines and other wastepaper; commingled metals, glass, and plastics; and garbage and other nonrecyclables. The newspaper, other paper wastes, and commingled recyclables are collected separately from the other refuse and are processed at a centralized material recycling facility, or MRF (pronounced "murf" in waste-management jargon). A modern MRF can process about 300 tons of recyclable wastes per day.

At a typical MRF, commingled recyclables are loaded onto a conveyor. Steel cans ("tin" cans are actually steel with only a thin coating of tin) are removed by an electromagnetic separator, and the remaining material passes over a vibrating screen in order to remove broken glass. Next, the conveyor passes through an air classifier, which separates aluminum and plastic containers from heavier glass containers. Glass is manually sorted by colour, and aluminum cans are separated from plastics by an eddy-current separator, which repels the aluminum from the conveyor belt.

FERROUS METALS

Ferrous products (i.e., iron and steel) can be recycled by both internal and external methods. Some internal recycling methods are obvious. Metal cuttings or imperfect products are recycled by remelting, recasting, and redrawing entirely within the steel mill. The process is much cheaper than producing new metal from the basic ore. Most iron and steel manufacturers produce their own coke. By-products from the coke oven include many organic compounds, hydrogen sulfide, and ammonia. The organic compounds are purified and sold. The ammonia is sold as an aqueous solution or combined with sulfuric acid to form ammonium sulfate, which is subsequently dried and sold as fertilizer.

In the ferrous metals industry there are also many applications of external recycling. Scrap steel makes up a significant percentage of the feed to electric arc and basic oxygen furnaces. The scrap comes from a variety of manufacturing operations that use steel as a basic material and from discarded or obsolete goods made from iron and steel. One of the largest sources of scrap steel is the reprocessing of old automobile bodies.

Salvage operations on automobiles actually begin before they reach the reprocessor. Parts such as transmissions and electrical components can be rebuilt and resold, and the engine block is removed and melted down for recasting.

After being crushed and flattened, the automobile body is shredded into small pieces by hammer mills. Ferrous metals are separated from the shredder residue by powerful magnets, while other materials are sorted out by hand or by jets of air. Only the plastics, textiles, and rubber from the residue are not reused. The same basic recovery procedures apply to washing machines, refrigerators, and other large, bulky steel or iron items. Lighter items such as steel cans are also recycled in large numbers.

Nonferrous Metals

At present, manual sorting seems to be the only practical method of separating pieces of nonferrous scrap materials such as aluminum, copper, and lead.

Secondary aluminum reprocessing is a large industry, involving the recycling of machine turnings, rejected castings, siding, and even aluminum covered with decorative plastic. The items are thrown into a reverberatory furnace (in which heat is radiated from the roof into the material treated) and melted while the impurities are burned off. The resulting material is cast into ingots and resold for drawing or forming operations. Beverage cans are another major source of recycled aluminum; in some countries, as many as two-thirds of all such cans are recycled.

The primary source of used lead is discarded electric storage batteries. Battery plates may be smelted to produce antimonial lead (a lead-antimony alloy) for manufacture of new batteries or to produce pure lead and antimony as separate products.

Rubber

Though much used rubber was formerly burned, this practice has been greatly curtailed in most countries in order to prevent air pollution. Internal recycling is common in most rubber plants. The reprocessed product can be used wherever premium-grade rubber is not needed. External recycling has proved a problem over the years, as the cost of recycling old or worn-out tires has far exceeded the value of the reclaimed material. Shredded rubber can be used as an additive in asphalt pavements, and discarded tires may be used as components of swings and other assorted recreational climbing equipment in "tire playgrounds" for children.

Paper and Other Cellulose Products

One of the most readily available materials for recycling is paper, which alone accounts for more than one-third by weight of all the material deposited in landfills in the United States. The stream of wastepaper consists principally of newspaper; office, copying, and writing paper; computer paper; coloured paper; paper tissues and towels; boxboard (used for cereal and other small boxes); corrugated cardboard; and kraft paper (used for paper bags). These papers must usually be sorted before recycling. Newsprint and cardboard can be repulped to make the same materials, while other types of scrap paper are recycled for use in low-quality papers such as boxboard, tissues, and towels. Paper intended for printing-grade products must be de-inked (often using caustic soda) after pulping; for some uses the stock is bleached before pressing into sheets. Smaller amounts of recycled paper are made into cellulose insulation and other building products.

Bark, wood chips, and lignin from sawmills, pulp mills, and paper mills are returned to the soil as fertilizers and soil conditioners. The kraft process of papermaking produces a variety of liquid wastes that are sources of such valuable chemicals as turpentine, methyl alcohol, dimethyl sulfide, ethyl alcohol, and acetone. Sludges from pulp and paper manufacture and phosphate slime from fertilizer manufacture can be made into wallboard.

GLASS

Glass makes up about 6 percent by weight of the material in municipal waste streams. Glass is an easily salvageable material but one that is difficult to recover economically. Though enormous numbers of glass containers are used throughout the world, much of this glass is still not recycled, because the raw materials are so inexpensive that there is scant economic motive to reuse them. Even those glass containers that are returned by consumers in their original form sooner or later become damaged or broken.

One problem in recycling glass is separating it from other refuse. Another problem is that waste glass must be separated by colour (i.e., clear, green, and brown) before it can be reused to make new glass containers. Despite these difficulties, anywhere from 35 to 90 percent of cullet (broken or refuse glass) is currently used in new-glass production, depending on the country.

PLASTICS

Plastics account for almost 10 percent by weight of the content of municipal garbage. Plastic containers and other household products are increasingly recycled, and, like paper, these must be sorted at the source before processing. Various thermoplastics may be remelted and reformed into new products.

Thermoplastics must be sorted by type before they can be remelted. Thermosetting plastics such as polyurethane and epoxy resins, by contrast, cannot be remelted; these are usually ground or shredded for use as fillers or insulating materials. So-called biodegradable plastics include starches that degrade upon exposure to sunlight (photodegradation), but a fine plastic residue remains, and the degradable additives preclude recycling of these products.

CONSTRUCTION AND DEMOLITION WASTE

Construction and demolition (C&D) debris (e.g., wood, brick, portland cement concrete, asphalt concrete and metals) can be reclaimed and reused to help reduce the volume taken up by such materials in landfills. Concrete debris consists mostly of sand and gravel that can be crushed and reused for road subbase gravel. Clean wood from C&D debris can be chipped and used as mulch, animal bedding, and fuel. Asphalt can be reused in cold-mix paving products and roofing shingles. Recovered wallboard can be used as cat litter. As landfill space becomes more expensive, more of these materials are being recycled.

DOMESTIC REFUSE

Domestic refuse (municipal solid waste) includes garbage (e.g., kitchen scraps) and rubbish (dry, nonputrescible refuse). Once glass, plastics, paper products, and metals have been removed from domestic refuse, what remains is essentially organic waste. This waste can be biologically decomposed and turned into humus, which is a useful soil conditioner, and kitchen scraps, when decomposed with leaves and grass in a compost mound, make an especially useful soil amendment. These practices help reduce the amount of material contributed by households to landfills.

CHAPTER 6
POLLUTION IN THE WATER

Water pollution is the release of substances into subsurface groundwater or into lakes, streams, rivers, estuaries, and oceans to the point where they interfere with beneficial use of the water or with the natural functioning of ecosystems. In addition to the release of substances such as chemicals or microorganisms, water pollution may also include the release of energy, in the form of radioactivity or heat, into bodies of water.

General types of water pollutants include pathogenic organisms, oxygen-demanding wastes, plant nutrients, synthetic organic chemicals, inorganic chemicals, sediments, radioactive substances, oil, and heat. Sewage is the primary source of the first three types. Farms and industrial facilities are also sources of some water pollutants. Sediment from eroded topsoil is considered a pollutant because it can damage aquatic ecosystems, and heat (particularly from power-plant cooling water) is considered a pollutant because of the adverse effect it has on dissolved oxygen levels and aquatic life in rivers and lakes.

Water pollutants may originate from point sources or from dispersed sources. A point-source pollutant is one that reaches water from a single pipeline or channel, such as a sewage discharge or outfall pipe. Dispersed sources are broad, unconfined areas from which pollutants enter a body of water. Surface runoff from farms, for example, is a dispersed source of pollution, carrying animal wastes, fertilizers, pesticides, and silt into nearby streams. Urban storm water drainage—which may carry sand and other gritty materials, petroleum residues from automobiles, and road deicing chemicals—is also considered a dispersed source because of the many locations at which it enters local streams or lakes.

Point-source pollutants are easier to control than dispersed-source pollutants, since they flow to a single location where treatment processes can remove them from the water. Such control is not usually possible over pollutants from dispersed sources, which cause a large part of the overall water pollution problem despite much progress in the building of modern sewage-treatment plants. Dispersed-source water pollution is best reduced by enforcing proper land-use plans and development standards.

THREATENED FRESHWATER

Water is present in abundant quantities on and under the Earth's surface, but most of Earth's estimated 1.4 billion cubic km (326 million cubic miles) of water is in the oceans or frozen in polar ice caps and glaciers. Ocean water contains about 35 grams per litre (4.5 ounces per gallon) of dissolved minerals or salts, making it unfit for drinking and for most industrial or agricultural uses. Less than 1 percent of Earth's water is liquid fresh water—water containing less than 3 grams of salts per litre, or less than one-eighth ounce of salts per gallon.

Nevertheless, there is ample fresh water on Earth to satisfy all human needs. It is not always available, though, at the times and places it is needed, and it is not uniformly distributed over the Earth. In many locations the availability of good-quality water is further reduced because of urban development, industrial growth, and environmental pollution.

Surface water and groundwater are both important sources for community water supply needs. Groundwater is a common source for single homes and small towns, and rivers and lakes are the usual sources for large cities.

THE HYDROLOGIC CYCLE

Water is in constant circulation, powered by the energy from sunlight and gravity in a natural process called the hydrologic cycle. Water evaporates from the ocean and land surfaces, is held temporarily as vapour in the atmosphere, and falls back to the Earth's surface as precipitation. Surface water is the residue of precipitation and melted snow, called runoff. Where the average rate of precipitation exceeds the rate at which runoff seeps into the soil, evaporates, or is absorbed by vegetation, bodies of surface water such as streams, rivers, and lakes are formed. Water that infiltrates the Earth's surface becomes groundwater, slowly seeping downward into extensive layers of porous soil and rock called aquifers. Under the pull of gravity, groundwater flows slowly and steadily through the aquifer.

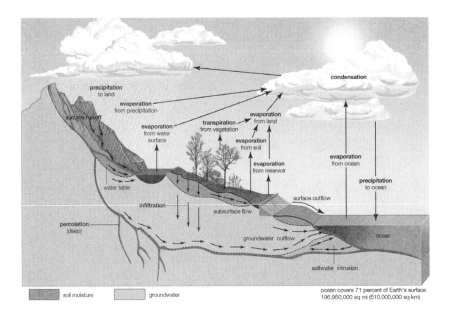

In the hydrologic cycle, water is transferred between the land surface, the ocean, and the atmosphere. The numbers on the arrows indicate relative water fluxes. Encyclopædia Britannica, Inc.

In low areas it emerges in springs and streams. Both surface water and groundwater eventually return to the ocean, where evaporation replenishes the supply of atmospheric water vapour. Winds carry the moist air over land, precipitation occurs, and the hydrologic cycle continues.

The activities of modern society are having a severe impact on the hydrologic cycle. The dynamic steady state is being disturbed by the discharge of toxic chemicals, radioactive substances, and other industrial wastes and by the seepage of mineral fertilizers, herbicides, and pesticides into surface and subsurface aquatic systems. Inadvertent and deliberate discharge of petroleum, improper sewage disposal, and thermal pollution also are seriously affecting the quality of the hydrosphere. Three major problems—eutrophication, acid rain, and the buildup of greenhouse gases—exemplify the far-reaching effects of human interference in the hydrologic cycle.

EUTROPHICATION

Historically, aquatic systems have been classified as oligotrophic or eutrophic. Oligotrophic waters are poorly fed by the nutrients nitrogen and phosphorus and have low concentrations of these constituents. There is thus low production of organic matter by photosynthesis in such waters. By contrast, eutrophic waters are well supplied with nutrients and generally have high concentrations of nitrogen and phosphorus and, correspondingly, large concentrations of plankton owing to high biological productivity. The waters of such aquatic systems are usually murky, and lakes and coastal marine systems may be oxygen-depleted at depth.

The process of eutrophication is defined as high biological productivity resulting from increased input of nutrients or organic matter into aquatic systems. For lakes, this increased biological productivity usually leads to decreased lake volume because of the accumulation of organic detritus. Natural eutrophication occurs as aquatic systems fill in with organic matter; it is distinct from cultural eutrophication, which is caused by human intervention. The latter is characteristic of aquatic systems that have been artificially enriched by excess nutrients and organic matter from sewage, agriculture, and industry. Naturally eutrophic lakes may produce 75–250 grams of carbon per square metre per year, whereas those lakes experiencing eutrophication because of human activities can support 75–750 grams per square metre per year. Commonly, culturally eutrophic aquatic systems may exhibit extremely low oxygen concentrations in bottom waters. This is particularly true of stratified systems, as, for instance, lakes during summer where concentrations of molecular oxygen may reach levels of less than about one milligram per litre—a threshold for various biological and chemical processes.

Aquatic systems may change from oligotrophic to eutrophic, or the rate of eutrophication of a natural eutrophic system may be accelerated by the addition of nutrients and organic matter due to human activities. The process of cultural eutrophication, however, can be reversed by shutting off the excess nutrient and organic matter supply.

The Effect of Acid Rain on Freshwater Aquatic Systems

The emission of sulfur dioxide and nitrogen oxides to the atmosphere by human activities—primarily fossil-fuel burning—has led to the acidification of rain and freshwater aquatic systems. Acid rain is a worldwide problem affecting many populated regions.

Acid rain is defined as precipitation with a pH of 5.6 or lower that results from reactions involving gases other than carbon dioxide. Low pH values are a result of equili-bration of rainwater with the atmospheric acid gases of carbon, nitrogen, and sulfur. (Equilibration only with atmospheric carbon dioxide would give a pH of 5.7.) The significantly lower values seen in acid rain are a result of reactions with nitrogen- and sulfur-bearing gaseous atmo-spheric components derived primarily from fossil-fuel burning sources.

The processes that remove anthropogenic emissions of sulfur dioxide and nitrogen oxides from the atmosphere also remove the hydrogen ion produced in the rain by the oxidation and hydrolysis of these acid gases. This excess hydrogen ion can bring about the acidification of freshwa-ter aquatic systems, particularly those with little buffer capacity (e.g., lakes situated in crystalline rock terrains). Furthermore, the lower pH values of rainwater, and con-sequently of soil water, can lead to increased mobilization of aluminum from rocks broken down by acid precipita-tion. Acidification of freshwater lakes in the eastern United States and increased aluminum concentrations in their waters are thought to be responsible for major changes in the ecosystems of the lakes. In particular, many lakes of this region lack substantial fish populations today, even though they supported large numbers of fish in the early 1900s.

GREENHOUSE GASES AND THE HYDROLOGIC CYCLE

One problem brought about by human action that is definitely affecting the hydrosphere globally is that of the greenhouse gases emitted to the atmosphere. Of the greenhouse gases released by anthropogenic activities, carbon dioxide has received the most attention. It has been shown by various measurement techniques that the present atmospheric concentration of carbon of more than 380 ppm is more than one-third higher than its late-1700s value. Much of this increase is due to carbon dioxide released to the atmosphere from the burning of coal, oil, gas, and wood and from deforestation practices (as, for example, those adopted in the Amazon River basin).

Instrumental climate records indicate that, over the past century, there has been a rise in global surface temperature of 0.6 °C (1.1 °F), an associated elevation of global sea level of 17 cm (6.7 inches), and a decrease in snow cover in the Northern Hemisphere of approximately 1.5 million square km (580,000 square miles). Based on greenhouse climate models where civilization continues to burn fossil fuels at early 21st-century rates, it is possible that atmospheric carbon dioxide concentrations will double their current level by the end of the 21st century, and these higher levels, along with those of other greenhouse gases (e.g., methane and nitrous oxide), will give rise to a further global mean surface temperature increase of 1.8 to 4.0 °C (3.2 to 7.2 °F). This projected temperature increase would be greater at the poles than at the equator and greater in the Arctic than in the Antarctic.

The effect of such a rise in surface temperature would be to speed up the hydrologic cycle and probably the rate of chemical weathering of continental rocks. The effect on the water balance would be regional in nature, with some places becoming wetter and others drier. In general, there would be a trend toward greater and longer periods of summer dryness induced by lower soil moisture content and higher evaporation rates in the mid-latitudes of the Northern Hemisphere. In the arid western regions of the United States, which depend on irrigation for growing plants, severe water shortages could occur. By contrast, precipitation and runoff might increase, except in summer, at latitudes beyond 60° N because of a greater poleward transport of moisture.

Global warming could further affect the hydrologic cycle by the melting of mountain glaciers, resulting in the transfer of water to the oceans. This process, together with thermal expansion of the oceans because of global warming, could lead to a slow rise in sea level of 0.21 to 0.48 metre (0.7 to 1.6 ft) by 2100. Melting of the Greenland Ice Sheet would add another 5 to 6 metres (16 to 20 ft) to predicted sea-level rise, and if the West Antarctic ice sheet were to disintegrate, additional sea-level rise would approach 10.5 metres (34 ft) over the next several hundred years. It is also possible that global warming has contributed to a documented reduction in the areal extent and thickness of sea ice in the Arctic and Antarctic regions.

The potential changes in the hydrologic cycle induced by a global warming could have severe consequences for ecosystems and human populations, especially since the latter are so sensitive to and dependent on such changes.

A lone fisherman motors his way through Greenland's Ice Fjord of Ilulissat. Global warming caused by greenhouse gases could melt the Greenland Ice Sheet even further, resulting in raised sea levels. AFP/Getty Images

A global rise in sea level of one metre, for example, would almost completely inundate the coastal areas of Bangladesh. Island nations and continental beaches and cities would be endangered. Agricultural lands could be displaced, just as patterns of arid, semiarid, and wet lands might become modified. It is essential that society plan for such potential changes so that, if they do occur, appropriate adjustments can be made to accommodate them.

Surface Waters

The total land area that contributes surface runoff to a river or lake is called a watershed, drainage basin, or catchment area. The volume of water available for municipal supply depends mostly on the amount of rainfall. It also depends on the size of the watershed, the slope of the ground, the type of soil and vegetation, and the type of land use.

Reservoirs

The flow rate or discharge of a river varies with time. Higher flow rates typically occur in the spring, and lower flow rates occur in the winter. When the average discharge of a river is not enough for a dependable supply of water, a conservation reservoir may be built. The flow of water is blocked by a dam, allowing an artificial lake to be formed. Conservation reservoirs store water from wet weather periods for use during times of drought and low streamflow. A water intake structure is built within the reservoir, with inlet ports and valves at several depths. Since the quality of water in a reservoir varies seasonally with depth, a multilevel intake allows water of best quality to be withdrawn.

When streamflow is impounded in a reservoir, the flow velocity decreases and sediment is deposited. Thus,

The primary water reservoir of São Paulo, Brazil. Caio do Valle

streams that transport much suspended sediment are poor sites for reservoirs; siltation will rapidly reduce storage capacity and severely shorten the useful life of a small reservoir. Even in larger reservoirs, sedimentation constitutes a common and serious problem. Because removal of the deposited sediments from reservoirs is generally too costly to be practical, reservoirs on a sediment-laden stream are characteristically planned to provide a reserve of storage capacity to offset the depletion caused by sedimentation. Despite this, the life expectancy of most reservoirs does not exceed 100 years at present sedimentation rates.

An associated problem is erosion of the stream channel below a reservoir when water is released. Because the sediment load is deposited in the reservoir, the released water has renewed transporting capacity, and channel erosion results.

Water in a reservoir may be lost by surface evaporation, by seepage into the surrounding soil or rocks, and by seepage through dam foundations. Seepage losses ordinarily can be reduced, but evaporation losses are often of major consequence. Gross evaporation from water surfaces in the temperate and tropical climates may amount to a few metres a year. In humid regions this loss is offset by direct precipitation, and the net surface loss may be moderate or negligible. In regions of lower rainfall the net loss may be substantial, amounting to 1.5 metres (5 ft) or more annually in some desert areas.

Water reservoirs range in size and complexity from small single-purpose impoundments to huge and complex multiple-purpose impoundments. A single-purpose reservoir is designed to fulfill only one function, such as irrigation, power generation, navigation, flood control, water supply, recreation, or low-flow regulation. The trend has been toward construction of multiple-purpose reservoirs designed to serve at least two principal functions.

Reservoirs can cause adverse environmental impacts — e.g., destruction of fish habitats and ecosystems)—and large-scale reservoir projects may require the submergence of cities and towns. For example, construction of the Three Gorges Dam on the Yangtze River (Chang Jiang) in China, designed primarily for flood control and as a source of electric power, displaced almost two million people from their homes. Social and environmental impacts must be taken into account during the planning stages of new reservoirs.

SURFACE WATER POLLUTANTS

Water bodies can be polluted by a wide variety of substances, including pathogenic microorganisms, putrescible organic waste, plant nutrients, toxic chemicals, sediments, heat, oil, and radioactive substances.

Domestic sewage is the primary source of pathogens (disease-causing microorganisms) and putrescible organic

Algal bloom caused by Euglena *algae.* Encyclopædia Britannica, Inc.

substances. Because pathogens are excreted in feces, all sewage from cities and towns is likely to contain pathogens of some type, potentially presenting a direct threat to public health. Putrescible organic matter presents a different sort of threat to water quality. As organics are decomposed naturally in the sewage by bacteria and other microorganisms, the dissolved oxygen content of the water is depleted. This endangers the quality of lakes and streams, where high levels of oxygen are required for fish and other aquatic organisms to survive. Sewage-treatment processes reduce the levels of pathogens and organics in wastewater, but they do not eliminate them completely.

Domestic sewage is also a major source of plant nutrients, mainly nitrates and phosphates. Excess nitrates and phosphates in water promote the growth of algae, sometimes causing unusually dense and rapid growths known as algal blooms. When the algae die, they add to the organic substances already present in the water; eventually, the water becomes even more deficient in oxygen. Anaerobic organisms (organisms that do not require oxygen to live) then attack the organic wastes, releasing gases such as methane and hydrogen sulfide, which are harmful to the aerobic (oxygen-requiring) forms of life. The result is a foul-smelling, oxygen-deficient, waste-filled body of water, as described above in the section on eutrophication. Eutrophication is a naturally occurring, slow, and inevitable process. However, when it is accelerated by human activity and water pollution (a phenomenon called cultural eutrophication), it can lead to the premature aging and death of a body of water.

Sources of toxic chemicals include improperly disposed wastewater from industrial plants and chemical process facilities (lead, mercury, chromium) as well as surface runoff containing pesticides used on agricultural areas and suburban lawns (chlordane, dieldrin, heptachlor).

Sediment (e.g., silt) resulting from soil erosion can be carried into water bodies by surface runoff from construction sites. Suspended sediment interferes with the penetration of sunlight and upsets the ecological balance of a body of water. Also, it can disrupt the reproductive cycles of fish and other forms of life, and when it settles out of suspension it can smother bottom-dwelling organisms.

Heat is considered to be a water pollutant because it decreases the capacity of water to hold dissolved oxygen in solution, and it increases the rate of metabolism of fish. Valuable species of game fish (e.g., trout) cannot survive in water with very low levels of dissolved oxygen. A major source of heat is the practice of discharging cooling water from power plants into rivers; the discharged water may be as much as 15 °C (27 °F) warmer than the naturally occurring water. This is called thermal pollution.

Finally, oil pollution occurs when oil from roads and parking lots is carried in surface runoff into water bodies.

GROUNDWATERS

Groundwater—water contained in underground geologic formations called aquifers—is a source of drinking water for many people. For example, about half the people in the United States depend on groundwater for their domestic water supply. Although approximately 98 percent of liquid fresh water exists as groundwater, much of it occurs very deep in the Earth. This makes pumping very expensive, preventing the full development and use of all groundwater resources.

AQUIFERS

The value of an aquifer as a source of groundwater is a function of the porosity of the geologic stratum, or layer, of which it is formed. Water is withdrawn from an aquifer by pumping it out of a well or infiltration gallery. An infiltration gallery typically includes several horizontal perforated pipes radiating outward from the bottom of a large-diameter vertical shaft. Wells are constructed in several ways, depending on the depth and nature of the aquifer. Wells used for public water supplies, usually more than 30 metres (100 ft) deep and from 10 to 30 cm (4 to 12 inches) in diameter, must penetrate large aquifers that can provide dependable yields of good-quality water. They are drilled using impact or rotary techniques and are usually lined with a metal pipe or casing to prevent contamination. The annular space around the outside of the upper portion of the casing is filled with cement grout, and a special sanitary seal is installed at the top to provide further protection. At the bottom of the casing, a slotted screen is attached to strain silt and sand out of the groundwater. A submersible pump driven by an electric motor can be used to raise the water to the surface. Sometimes a deep well may penetrate a confined artesian aquifer, in which case natural hydrostatic pressure can raise the water to the surface as an artesian well.

POLLUTION OF GROUNDWATER

Although groundwater may appear crystal clear (due to the natural filtration that occurs as it flows slowly through layers of soil), it may still be polluted by dissolved chemicals and by bacteria and viruses. Sources of chemical contaminants include poorly designed or poorly maintained subsurface sewage-disposal systems (e.g., septic tanks), industrial wastes disposed of in improperly lined or unlined landfills or lagoons, leachates from unlined municipal refuse landfills, and mining and petroleum production activities. In coastal areas, increasing withdrawal of groundwater (due to urbanization and

ARTESIAN WELLS

An artesian well is a well from which water flows under natural pressure without pumping. It is dug or drilled wherever a gently dipping, permeable rock layer (such as sandstone) receives water along its outcrop at a level higher than the level of the surface of the ground at the well site. At the outcrop the water moves down into the aquifer (water-bearing layer) but is prevented from leaving it, by impermeable rock layers (such as shale) above and below it. Pressure from the water's weight (hydrostatic pressure) forces water to the surface of a well drilled down into the aquifer; the pressure for the steady upflow is maintained by the continuing penetration of water into the aquifer at the intake area.

In places where the overlying impermeable rocks are broken by joints or faults, water may escape through them to rise to the surface as artesian springs. In some areas, artesian wells and springs are a major source of water, especially in arid plains adjacent to mountain ranges that receive precipitation. The rapid development of new wells through over-drilling, however, has tended to reduce head pressures in many artesian systems. As a result, most artesian wells are now outfitted with pumps.

industrialization) can cause saltwater intrusion; as the water table drops, seawater is drawn into wells.

THREATENED OCEANS

Although estuaries and oceans contain vast volumes of water, their natural capacity to absorb pollutants is limited. Contamination from sewage outfall pipes, from dumping of sludge or other wastes, and from oil spills can harm marine life, especially microscopic phytoplankton that serve as food for larger aquatic organisms. Sometimes, unsightly and dangerous waste materials can be washed back to shore, littering beaches with hazardous debris. It is estimated that roughly 25,000 metric tons (55 million pounds) of discarded bottles, cans, and plastic containers are dumped at sea each year. In the United States the dumping of sludge and solid waste has been banned in all coastal areas.

EUTROPHICATION AND DEAD ZONES

Coastal marine systems may be affected by the same process of cultural eutrophication that affects many freshwater aquatic systems. On a global scale, the input by rivers of organic matter to the oceans today is twice the input in prehuman times, and the flux of nitrogen, together with that of phosphorus, has more than doubled. This excess loading of carbon, nitrogen, and phosphorus is leading to cultural eutrophication of marine systems. In several polluted eastern U.S. estuaries and in some estuaries of Europe (e.g., the Scheldt of Belgium and The Netherlands), all of the dissolved silica brought into the estuarine waters by rivers is removed by phytoplankton growth (primarily diatoms) resulting from excess fluxes of nutrients and organic matter. In the North Sea, there is now a deficiency of silica and an excess of nitrogen and phosphorus, which in turn has led to a decrease in diatom productivity and an increase in cyanobacteria productivity—a biotic change brought about by cultural eutrophication.

Another ocean pollution problem is the seasonal formation in certain coastal areas of "dead zones" (i.e., hypoxic areas, where dissolved oxygen levels drop so low that most higher forms of aquatic life vanish). The cause is nutrient enrichment from dispersed agricultural runoff and concomitant algal blooms. Dead zones occur worldwide; one of the largest of these (sometimes as large as 22,000 square km, or 8,500 square miles) forms annually in the Gulf of Mexico, beginning at the Mississippi River delta.

OIL SPILLS

Accidental oceanic oil spills became a major environmental problem in the 1960s and 70s, chiefly as a result of intensified petroleum exploration and production on continental shelves and the use of supertankers capable of transporting more than 500,000 tons of oil. Two enormously important oil-tanker spills that took place in European waters were the *Torrey Canyon* disaster off Cornwall, England, in 1967 (119,000 tons of crude oil were spilled) and the *Amoco Cadiz* disaster off Brittany, France, in 1978 (223,000 tons of crude oil and ship fuel were spilled). Both events led to lasting changes in the regulation of shipping and in the organization of responses to ecological emergencies such as oil spills.

Spectacular oil spills from wrecked or damaged supertankers are now rare, because of stringent shipping and environmental regulations. Nevertheless, thousands of minor and several major oil spills related to well discharges and tanker operations are reported each year, with the total quantity of oil released annually into the world's oceans exceeding 1 million tons. The unintentional or negligent release of used gasoline solvents and crankcase lubricants by industries and individuals greatly aggravates the overall environmental problem. Combined with natural seepage from the ocean floor, these sources add oil to the world's waterways at the rate of 3.5 to 6 million tons a year.

OIL-SPILL DAMAGE

The costs of oil spills are considerable in both economic and ecological terms. Oil on ocean surfaces is harmful to many

THE EXXON VALDEZ

On March 24, 1989, the United States suffered what was, at the time, the worst oil pollution incident in its history when an Exxon Corporation tanker, the *Exxon Valdez*, ran aground on Bligh Reef in Prince William Sound, an inlet in the Gulf of Alaska, and spilled nearly 11 million gallons (41 million litres) of North Slope crude oil across the sound. The ship was later refloated and towed away for repairs, but bad weather and delays in the arrival of suitable equipment hampered efforts to contain the spilled oil. The spill eventually polluted 1,300 miles (2,100 kilometres) of indented shoreline, as well as adjacent waters, as far south as the southern end of Shelikof Strait between Kodiak Island and the Alaska Peninsula. Thousands of workers and volunteers helped to clean up after the oil spill, and Exxon provided $2.1 billion in funding. Despite these cleanup efforts, the spill exterminated much native wildlife, including salmon, herring, sea otters, bald eagles, and killer whales.

The National Transportation Safety Board (NTSB) eventually assigned most of the blame for the oil spill to Exxon, citing its incompetent and overworked crew. The board also faulted the U.S. Coast Guard for an inadequate system of traffic regulation. After evidence suggested that the ship's captain had been drinking before the accident, Exxon terminated his employment. The *Exxon Valdez* itself was repaired and recommissioned but was legally prohibited from ever reentering Prince William Sound.

forms of aquatic life because it prevents sufficient amounts of sunlight from penetrating the surface, and also reduces the level of dissolved oxygen. Crude oil ruins the insulating and waterproofing properties of feathers and fur, and thus oil-coated birds and marine mammals may die from hypothermia. Moreover, ingested oil can be toxic to affected animals, and damage to their habitat and reproductive rate may slow the long-term recovery of animal populations from the short-term damage caused by the spill itself.

Damage to plant life can be considerable as well. Saltwater marshes and mangroves are two notable shore ecosystems that frequently suffer from oil spills. If beaches and populated shorelines are fouled, tourism and commerce may be severely affected, as may power plants and other utilities that either draw on or discharge into seawater at the shore. One of the industries most affected by oil spills is fishing. Major oil spills are frequently followed by the immediate suspension of commercial fishing, at the least to prevent damage to vessels and equipment but also to prevent the catch and sale of fish or shellfish that may be contaminated.

The immediate environmental effects of oil spills have been readily identified, but their long-term impact on the ecological system of an affected area is more difficult to assess. The cost of paying compensation to individuals and communities damaged by oil spills has been a major incentive to reduce the chances of such events taking place in the future.

Oil-Spill Cleanup

As yet, no thoroughly satisfactory method has been developed for cleaning up major oil spills, though the spectacular spills of the last decades of the 20th century called forth great improvements in technology and in the management of coordinated responses. Essentially, responses to oil spills seek to contain the oil and remove enough of it so that economic activity can resume and the natural recovery processes of the marine environment can take over. Floating booms can be placed around the source of the spill or at entrances to channels and harbours to reduce the spreading of an oil slick over the sea surface. Skimming, a technique that, like the use of booms, is most effective in calm waters, involves various mechanisms that physically separate the oil from the water and place the oil into collection tanks.

Another approach is to use various sorbents (e.g., straw, volcanic ash, and shavings of polyester-derived plastic) that absorb the oil from the water. Where appropriate, chemical surfactants and solvents may be spread over a slick in order to accelerate its natural dispersion into the sea. Onshore removal of oil that has penetrated sandy beaches and coated rocky shores is a laborious affair, frequently involving small armies of workers wielding hand tools or operating heavy construction-type equipment to scrape up contaminated debris and haul it away.

MUNICIPAL WATER CONSUMPTION

Water consumption in a community is characterized by several types of demand, including domestic, public, commercial, and industrial uses. Domestic demand includes water for drinking, cooking, washing, laundering, and other household functions. Public demand includes water for fire protection, street cleaning, and use in schools and

A worker uses absorbent material to extract oil from shoreline waters in Muxia, Spain, after a 2002 tanker spill. Marco Di Lauro/Getty Images

other public buildings. Commercial and industrial demands include water for stores, offices, hotels, laundries, restaurants, and most manufacturing plants. There is usually a wide variation in total water demand among different communities. This variation depends on population, geographic location, climate, the extent of local commercial and industrial activity, and the cost of water.

Water use or demand is expressed numerically by average daily consumption per capita (per person). In the United States the average is approximately 380 litres (100 gallons) per capita per day for domestic and public needs. Overall, the average total demand is about 680 litres (180 gallons) per capita per day, when commercial and industrial water uses are included. (These figures do not include withdrawals from freshwater sources for such purposes as crop irrigation or cooling operations at electric power-generating facilities.) Water consumption in some developing countries may average as little as 15 litres (4 gallons) per capita per day. The world average is estimated to be approximately 60 litres (16 gallons) per person per day.

In any community, water demand varies on a seasonal, daily, and hourly basis. On a hot summer day, for example, it is not unusual for total water consumption to be as much as 200 percent of the average demand. The peak demands in residential areas usually occur in the morning and early evening hours (just before and after the normal workday). Water demands in commercial and industrial districts, though, are usually uniform during the work day. Minimum water demands typically occur in the very early or predawn morning hours. Civil and environmental engineers must carefully study each community's water use patterns in order to design efficient pumping and distribution systems.

Although pure water is rarely found in nature (because of the strong tendency of water to dissolve other substances), the characterization of water quality (i.e., clean or polluted) is a function of the intended use of the water. For example, water that is clean enough for swimming and fishing may not be clean enough for drinking and cooking. Water quality standards (limits on the amount of impurities allowed in water intended for a particular use) provide a legal framework for the prevention of water pollution of all types. There are several types of water quality standards. Stream standards are those that classify streams, rivers, and lakes on the basis of their maximum beneficial use; they set allowable levels of specific substances or qualities (e.g., dissolved oxygen, turbidity, pH) allowed in those bodies of water, based on their given classification. Effluent standards set specific limits on the levels of contaminants (e.g., biochemical oxygen demand, suspended solids, nitrogen) allowed in the final discharges from wastewater-treatment plants. Drinking-water standards include limits on the levels of specific contaminants allowed in potable water delivered to homes for domestic use.

Drinking-Water Quality

Water has such a strong tendency to dissolve other substances that it is rarely found in nature in a pure condition. When it falls as rain, small amounts of gases such as oxygen and carbon dioxide become dissolved in it. Raindrops also carry tiny dust particles and other substances. As it flows over the ground, water picks up fine soil particles, microbes, organic material, and soluble minerals. In lakes, bogs, and swamps, water may gain colour, taste, and odour from decaying vegetation and other natural organic matter. Groundwater usually acquires more dissolved minerals than does surface runoff because of its longer direct contact with soil and rock. It may also absorb gases such as hydrogen sulfide and methane. In populated areas the quality of surface water as well as groundwater is directly influenced by human activities and the effects of pollution.

HEALTH CONCERNS

Five general types of impurities are of public health concern. These are organic chemicals, inorganic chemicals, turbidity, microorganisms, and radioactive substances. Organic contaminants include various pesticides, industrial solvents, and trihalomethanes such as chloroform. Inorganic contaminants of major concern include arsenic, nitrate, fluoride, and toxic metals such as lead and mercury. All these substances can harm human health when present above certain concentrations in drinking water. A low concentration of fluoride, however, has been proved to promote dental health. Some communities add fluoride to their water for this purpose.

Turbidity refers to cloudiness caused by very small particles of silt, clay, and other substances suspended in water. Even a slight degree of turbidity in drinking water is objectionable to most people. Turbidity also interferes with disinfection by creating a possible shield for pathogenic organisms. Groundwater normally has very low turbidity, because of the natural filtration that occurs as it percolates through the soil. Surface waters, though, are often high in turbidity.

The most important microbiological measure of drinking-water quality is a group of bacteria called coliforms. Coliform bacteria normally are not pathogenic, but they are always present in the intestinal tract of humans and are excreted in very large numbers with human waste. Water contaminated with human waste always contains coliforms, and it is also likely to contain pathogens excreted by infected individuals in the community. Since it is easier to test for the presence of coliforms rather than for specific types of pathogens, coliforms are used as indicator organisms for measuring the biological quality of water. If coliforms are not found in the water, it can be assumed that the water is also free of pathogens. The coliform count thus reflects the chance of pathogens being present; the lower the coliform count, the less likely it is that pathogens are in the water.

Radioactive materials from natural as well as industrial sources can be harmful water contaminants. Wastes from uranium mining, nuclear power plants, and medical research are possible pollutants. Strontium-90 and tritium are radioactive contaminants that have been found in water as a result of nuclear weapons testing. Naturally occurring substances such as radium and radon gas are found in some groundwater sources. The danger from dissolved radon gas arises not from drinking the water but from breathing the gas after it is released into the air.

Aesthetic Concerns

Colour, taste, and odour are physical characteristics of drinking water that are important for aesthetic reasons rather than for health reasons. Colour in water may be caused by decaying leaves or by algae, giving it a brownish yellow hue. Taste and odour may be caused by naturally occurring dissolved organics or gases. Some well-water supplies, for example, have a rotten-egg odour that is caused by hydrogen sulfide gas. Chemical impurities associated with the aesthetic quality of drinking water include iron, manganese, copper, zinc, and chloride. Dissolved metals impart a bitter taste to water and may stain laundry and plumbing fixtures. Excessive chlorides give the water an objectionable salty taste.

HARDNESS

Another parameter of water quality is hardness. This is a term used to describe the effect of dissolved minerals (mostly calcium and magnesium). Minerals cause deposits of scale in hot water pipes, and they also interfere with the lathering action of soap. Hard water does not harm human health, but the economic problems it causes make it objectionable to most people.

WATER QUALITY STANDARDS

Water quality standards set limits on the concentrations of impurities allowed in water. Standards also affect the selection of raw water sources and the choice of treatment processes. The development of water quality standards began in the United States in the early 20th century. Since that time, the total number of regulated contaminants has increased as toxicological knowledge and analytical measurement techniques have improved. Modern testing methods now allow the detection of contaminants in extremely low concentrations—as low as one part contaminant per one billion parts water or even, in some cases, per one trillion parts water. Water quality standards are continually evolving, usually becoming more stringent. As a result, the number of regulated contaminants increases over time, and their allowable concentrations in water are lowered.

Drinking-water regulations include two types of standards: primary and secondary. Primary standards are designed to protect public health, whereas secondary standards are based on aesthetic factors rather than on health effects. Primary standards specify maximum contaminant levels for many chemical, microbiological, and radiological parameters of water quality. They reflect the best available scientific and engineering judgment and take into account exposure from other sources in the environment and from foods. Turbidity is also included in the primary standards because of its tendency to interfere with disinfection. Secondary standards are guidelines or suggested maximum levels of colour, taste, odour, hardness, corrosiveness, and certain other factors.

MUNICIPAL WATER SUPPLY SYSTEMS

Municipal water supply systems transport water from areas of abundance to an area of shortage. They include works for the collection, transmission, treatment, storage, and distribution of water for homes, commercial establishments, industry, and irrigation, as well as for such public needs as firefighting and street flushing. The design of these facilities depends on the quality of the water, on the particular needs of the user or consumer, and on the quantities of water that must be processed. Of all municipal services, provision of potable water is perhaps the most vital. People depend on water for drinking, cooking, washing, carrying away wastes, and other domestic needs. Water supply systems must also meet requirements for public, commercial, and industrial activities. In all cases, the water must fulfill both quality and quantity requirements.

HISTORICAL DEVELOPMENT OF
WATER SUPPLY SYSTEMS

Water was an important factor in the location of the earliest settled communities, and the evolution of public water supply systems is tied directly to the growth of cities. In the development of water resources beyond their natural condition in rivers, lakes, and springs, the digging of shallow wells was probably the earliest innovation. As the need for water increased and tools were developed, wells were made deeper. Brick-lined wells were built by city dwellers in the Indus River basin as early as 2500 BCE, and wells almost 500 metres (more than 1,600 ft) deep are known to have been used in ancient China.

Construction of *qanāt*s, slightly sloping tunnels driven into hillsides that contained groundwater, probably originated in ancient Persia about 700 BCE. From the hillsides the water was conveyed by gravity in open channels to nearby towns or cities. The use of *qanāt*s became widespread throughout the region, and some are still in existence. Until 1933 the Iranian capital city, Tehran, drew its entire water supply from a system of *qanāt*s.

The need to channel water supplies from distant sources was an outcome of the growth of urban communities.

The remains of a defunct qanāt in Iran. This type of water supply system is believed to have originated in ancient Persia about 700 BCE. Shutterstock.com

Among the most notable of ancient water-conveyance systems are the aqueducts built between 312 BCE and 455 CE throughout the Roman Empire. Some of these impressive works are still in existence. The writings of Sextus Julius Frontinus (who was appointed superintendent of Roman aqueducts in 97 CE) provide information about the design and construction of the 11 major aqueducts that supplied Rome itself. Extending from a distant spring-fed area, a lake, or a river, a typical Roman aqueduct included a series of underground and aboveground channels. The longest was the Aqua Marcia, built in 144 BCE. Its source was about 37 km (23 miles) from Rome. The aqueduct itself was 92 km (57 miles) long, however, because it had to meander along land contours in order to maintain a steady flow of water. For about 80 km (50 miles) the aqueduct was underground in a covered trench, and only for the last 11 km (7 miles) was it carried aboveground on an arcade. In fact, most of the combined length of the aqueducts supplying Rome (about 420 km [260 miles]) was built as covered trenches or tunnels. When crossing a valley, aqueducts were supported by arcades comprising one or more levels of massive granite piers and impressive arches.

The aqueducts ended in Rome at distribution reservoirs, from which the water was conveyed to public baths or fountains. A few very wealthy or privileged citizens had water piped directly into their homes, but most of the people carried water in containers from a public fountain. Water was running constantly, the excess being used to clean the streets and flush the sewers.

Ancient aqueducts and pipelines were not capable of withstanding much pressure. Channels were constructed of cut stone, brick, rubble, or rough concrete. Pipes were typically made of drilled stone or of hollowed wooden logs, although clay and lead pipes were also used. During the Middle Ages there was no notable progress in the methods or materials used to convey and distribute water.

Cast-iron pipes with joints capable of withstanding high pressures were not used very much until the early 19th century. The steam engine was first applied to water-pumping operations at about that time, making it possible for all but the smallest communities to have drinking water supplied directly to individual homes. Asbestos cement, ductile iron, reinforced concrete, and steel came into use as materials for water supply pipelines in the 20th century.

MODERN WATER DISTRIBUTION SYSTEMS

A water distribution system is a network of pumps, pipelines, storage tanks, and other appurtenances. It must deliver adequate quantities of water at pressures sufficient for operating plumbing fixtures and firefighting equipment, yet it must not deliver water at pressures high enough to increase the occurrence of leaks and pipeline breaks. Pressure-regulating valves may be installed to reduce pressure levels in low-lying service areas. More than half the cost of a municipal water supply system is for the distribution network.

PIPELINES

The pipeline system of a municipal water distribution network consists of arterial water mains or primary feeders, which convey water from the treatment plant to areas of major water use in the community, and smaller-diameter pipelines called secondary feeders, which tie in to the mains. Usually not less than 150 mm (6 inches) in diameter, these pipelines are placed within the public right-of-way so that service connections can be made for all potential water users. The pipelines are usually arranged in a grid-iron pattern that allows water to circulate in interconnected loops; this permits any broken sections of pipe to be isolated for repair without disrupting service to large areas of the community. "Dead-end" patterns may also be used, but they do not permit circulation, and the water they provide is more susceptible to taste and odour problems because of stagnation.

A water distribution pipeline must be able to resist internal and external forces, as well as corrosion. Pipes are placed under stress by internal water pressure, by the weight of the overlying soil, and by vehicles passing above. They may have to withstand water-hammer forces; these occur when valves are closed too rapidly, causing pressure waves to surge through the system. In addition, metal pipes may rust internally if the water supply is corrosive or externally because of corrosive soil conditions.

Materials

Distribution pipes are made of asbestos cement, cast iron, ductile iron, plastic, reinforced concrete, or steel. Although not as strong as iron, asbestos cement, because of its corrosion resistance and ease of installation, is a desirable material for secondary feeders up to 41 cm (16 inches) in diameter. Pipe sections are easily joined with a coupling sleeve and rubber-ring gasket. Cast iron has an excellent record of service, with many installations still functioning after 100 years. Ductile iron, a stronger and more elastic type of cast iron, is used in newer installations. Iron pipes are provided in diameters up to 122 cm (48 inches) and are usually coated to prevent corrosion. Underground sections are connected with bell-and-spigot joints, the spigot end of one pipe section being pushed into the bell end of an adjacent section. A rubber-ring gasket in the bell end is compressed when the two sections are joined, creating a watertight, flexible connection. Flanged and bolted joints are used for aboveground installations.

Plastic pipes are available in diameters up to 61 cm (24 inches). They are lightweight, easily installed, and corrosion-resistant, and their smoothness provides good hydraulic characteristics. Plastic pipes are connected either by a bell-and-spigot compression-type joint or by threaded screw couplings.

Precast reinforced concrete pipe sections up to 366 cm (12 ft) in diameter are used for arterial mains. Reinforced concrete pipes are strong and durable. They are joined using a bell-and-spigot-type connection that is sealed with cement mortar. Steel pipe is sometimes used for arterial mains in aboveground installations. It is very strong and lighter than concrete pipe, but it must be protected against corrosion with lining of the interior and with painting and wrapping of the exterior. Sections of steel pipe are joined by welding or with mechanical coupling devices.

Fittings

In order to function properly, a water distribution system requires several types of fittings, including hydrants, shut-off valves, and other appurtenances. The main purpose of hydrants is to provide water for firefighting. They also are used for flushing water mains, pressure testing, water sampling, and washing debris off public streets.

Many types of valves are used to control the quantity and direction of water flow. Gate valves are usually installed throughout the pipe network. They allow sections to be shut off and isolated during the repair of broken mains, pumps, or hydrants. A type of valve commonly used for throttling and controlling the rate of flow is the butterfly valve. Other valves used in water distribution systems include pressure-reducing valves, check valves, and air-release valves.

Installation

Water mains must be placed roughly 1 to 2 metres (3 to 6 ft) below the ground surface in order to protect against traffic loads and to prevent freezing. Since the water in a distribution system is under pressure, pipelines can follow the shape of the land, uphill as well as downhill. They must be installed with proper bedding and backfill. Compaction of soil layers under the pipe (bedding) as well as above the pipe (backfill) is necessary to provide proper support. A water main should never be installed in the same trench with a sewer line. Where the two must cross, the water main should be placed above the sewer line.

PUMPS

Many kinds of pumps are used in distribution systems. Pumps that lift surface water and move it to a nearby treatment plant are called low-lift pumps. These move large volumes of water at relatively low discharge pressures. Pumps that discharge treated water into arterial mains are called high-lift pumps. These operate under higher pressures. Pumps that increase the pressure within the distribution system or raise water into an elevated storage tank are called booster pumps. Well pumps lift water from underground and discharge it directly into a distribution system.

Most water distribution pumps are of the centrifugal type, in which a rapidly rotating impeller adds energy to the water and raises the pressure inside the pump casing. The flow rate through a centrifugal pump depends on the pressure against which it operates. The higher the pressure, the lower the flow or discharge. Another kind of pump is the positive-displacement type. This pump delivers a fixed quantity of water with each cycle of a piston or rotor. The water is literally pushed or displaced from the pump casing. The flow capacity of a positive-displacement pump is unaffected by the pressure of the system in which it operates.

STORAGE TANKS

Distribution storage tanks, familiar sights in many communities, serve two basic purposes: equalizing storage and emergency storage. Equalizing storage is the volume of water needed to satisfy peak hourly demands in the community. During the late night and very early morning hours, when water demand is lower, high-lift pumps fill the tank. During the day, when water demand is higher, water flows out of the tank to help satisfy the peak hourly water needs. This allows for a uniform flow rate at the treatment plant and pumping station. The capacity of a distribution storage tank is about equal to the average daily water demand of the community.

Distribution storage tanks are built at ground level on hilltops higher than the service area. In areas with flat topography, the tanks may be elevated aboveground on towers in order to provide adequate water pressures, or ground-level storage tanks with booster pumping may be provided.

CHAPTER 7
WATER TREATMENT

Water in rivers or lakes is rarely clean enough for human consumption if it is not first treated or purified. Groundwater, too, often needs some level of treatment to render it potable. The primary objective of water treatment is to protect the health of the community. Potable water must, of course, be free of harmful microorganisms and chemicals, but public supplies should also be aesthetically desirable so that consumers will not be tempted to use water from another, more attractive but unprotected source. The water should be crystal clear, with almost no turbidity, and it should be free of objectionable colour, odour, and taste. For domestic supplies, water should not be corrosive, nor should it deposit troublesome amounts of scale and stains on plumbing fixtures. Industrial requirements may be even more stringent. Many industries provide special treatment on their own premises.

The type and extent of treatment required to obtain potable water depends on the quality of the source. The better the quality, the less treatment is needed. Surface water usually needs more extensive treatment than does groundwater, because most streams, rivers, and lakes are polluted to some extent. Even in areas remote from human populations, surface water contains suspended silt, organic material, decaying vegetation, and microbes from animal wastes. Groundwater, on the other hand, is usually free of microbes and suspended solids because of natural filtration as the water moves through soil, though it often contains relatively high concentrations of dissolved minerals from its direct contact with soil and rock.

Water is treated in a variety of physical and chemical methods. Treatment of surface water begins with intake

148

screens to prevent fish and debris from entering the plant and damaging pumps and other components. Conventional treatment of water primarily involves clarification and disinfection. In addition to clarification and disinfection, the processes of softening, aeration, carbon adsorption, and fluoridation may be used for certain public water sources. Desalination processes are used in areas where freshwater supplies are not readily available.

DEVELOPMENTS IN WATER TREATMENT

Even the ancients had an appreciation for the importance of water purity. Sanskrit writings from as early as 2000 BCE tell how to purify foul water by boiling and filtering. But it was not until the middle of the 19th century that a direct link between polluted water and disease (cholera) was proved, and it was not until the end of that same century that the German bacteriologist Robert Koch proved the germ theory of disease, establishing a scientific basis for the treatment and sanitation of drinking water.

Water treatment is the alteration of a water source in order to achieve a quality that meets specified goals. At the end of the 19th century and the beginning of the 20th, the main goal was elimination of deadly waterborne diseases. The treatment of public drinking water to remove pathogenic, or disease-causing, microorganisms began about that time. Treatment methods included sand filtration as well as the use of chlorine for disinfection. The virtual elimination of diseases such as cholera and typhoid in developed countries proved the success of this water-treatment technology. In developing countries, waterborne disease is still the principal water quality concern.

In industrialized countries, concern has shifted to the chronic health effects related to chemical contamination.

For example, trace amounts of certain synthetic organic substances in drinking water are suspected of causing cancer in humans. The added goal of reducing such health risks is seen in the continually increasing number of factors included in drinking-water standards.

CLARIFICATION

Clarification removes most of the turbidity, making the water crystal clear. Groundwater does not often need clarification, but it should be disinfected as a precaution to protect public health.

SEDIMENTATION

Impurities in water are either dissolved or suspended. The suspended material reduces clarity, and the easiest way to remove it is to rely on gravity. Under quiescent (still) conditions, suspended particles that are denser than water gradually settle to the bottom of a basin or tank. This is called plain sedimentation. Long-term water storage (for more than one month) in reservoirs reduces the amount of suspended sediment and bacteria. Nevertheless, additional clarification is usually needed. In a treatment plant, sedimentation (settling) tanks are built to provide a few hours of storage or detention time as the water slowly flows from tank inlet to outlet. It is impractical to keep water in the tanks for longer periods, because of the large volumes that must be treated.

Sedimentation tanks may be rectangular or circular in shape and are typically about 3 metres (10 ft) deep. Several tanks are usually provided and arranged for parallel (side-by-side) operation. Influent (water flowing in) is uniformly distributed as it enters a tank. Clarified effluent (water flowing out) is skimmed from the surface as it flows over

An older sedimentation tank in England. Modern tanks use a mechanized scraper to continuously and automatically remove sludge. Shutterstock.com

special baffles called weirs. The layer of concentrated solids that collects at the bottom of the tank is called sludge. Modern sedimentation tanks are equipped with mechanical scrapers that continuously push the sludge toward a collection hopper, where it is pumped out.

The efficiency of a sedimentation tank for removing suspended solids depends more on its surface area than on its depth or volume. A relatively shallow tank with a large surface area will be more effective than a very deep tank that holds the same volume but has a smaller surface area. Most sedimentation tanks, though, are not less than 3 metres deep, in order to provide enough room for a sludge layer and a scraper mechanism.

A technique called shallow-depth sedimentation is often applied in modern treatment plants. In this method, several prefabricated units or modules of "tube settlers" are installed near the tops of tanks in order to increase their effective surface area.

COAGULATION AND FLOCCULATION

Suspended particles cannot be removed completely by plain settling. Large, heavy particles settle out readily, but smaller and lighter particles settle very slowly or in some cases do not settle at all. Because of this, the sedimentation step is usually preceded by a chemical process known as coagulation. Chemicals (coagulants) are added to the water to bring the nonsettling particles together into larger, heavier masses of solids called floc. Aluminum sulfate (alum) is the most common coagulant used for water purification. Other chemicals, such as ferric sulfate or sodium aluminate, may also be used.

Coagulation is usually accomplished in two stages: rapid mixing and slow mixing. Rapid mixing serves to disperse the coagulants evenly throughout the water and to ensure a complete chemical reaction. Sometimes this is accomplished by adding the chemicals just before the pumps, allowing the pump impellers to do the mixing. Usually, though, a small flash-mix tank provides about one minute of detention time. After the flash mix, a longer period of gentle agitation is needed to promote particle collisions and enhance the growth of floc. This gentle agitation, or slow mixing, is called flocculation, which is accomplished in a tank that provides at least a half hour of detention time. The flocculation tank has wooden paddle-type mixers that slowly rotate on a horizontal motor-driven shaft. After flocculation the water flows into the sedimentation tanks. Some small water-treatment plants combine coagulation and sedimentation in a single prefabricated steel unit called a solids-contact tank.

FILTRATION

Even after coagulation and flocculation, sedimentation does not remove enough suspended impurities from water to make it crystal clear. The remaining nonsettling floc causes noticeable turbidity in the water and can shield microbes from disinfection. Filtration is a physical process that removes these impurities from water by percolating it downward through a layer or bed of porous, granular material such as sand. Suspended particles become trapped within the pore spaces of the filter media, which also remove harmful protozoa and natural colour. Most surface water supplies require filtration after the coagulation and sedimentation steps. For surface waters with low turbidity and colour, however, a process of direct filtration, which is not preceded by sedimentation, may be used.

Two types of sand filters are in use: slow and rapid. Slow filters require much more surface area than rapid filters and are difficult to clean. Most modern water-treatment plants now use rapid dual-media filters following coagulation and sedimentation. A dual-media filter consists of a layer of anthracite coal above a layer of fine sand. The upper layer of coal traps most of the large floc, and the finer sand grains in the lower layer trap smaller impurities. This process is called in-depth filtration, as the impurities are not simply screened out or removed at the surface of the filter bed, as is the case in slow sand filters. In order to enhance in-depth filtration, so-called mixed-media filters are used in some treatment plants. These have a third layer, consisting of a fine-grained dense mineral called garnet, at the bottom of the bed.

Rapid filters are housed in boxlike concrete structures, with multiple boxes arranged on both sides of a piping gallery. A large tank called a clear well is usually built under the filters to hold the clarified water temporarily. A layer of coarse gravel usually supports the filter media. When clogged by particles removed from the water, the filter bed must be cleaned by backwashing. In the backwash process, the direction of flow through the filter is reversed. Clean water is forced upward through the media, expanding the filter bed slightly and carrying away the impurities in wash troughs. The backwash water is distributed uniformly across the filter bottom by an underdrain system of perforated pipes or porous tile blocks.

Because of its reliability, the rapid filter is the most common type of filter used to treat public water supplies. However, other types of filters may be used, including pressure filters, diatomaceous earth filters, and microstrainers. A pressure filter has a granular media bed, but, instead of being open at the top like a gravity-flow rapid filter, it is enclosed in a cylindrical steel tank. Water is pumped through the filter under pressure. In diatomaceous earth filters, a natural powderlike material composed of the shells of microscopic organisms called diatoms is used as a filter media. The powder is supported in a thin layer on a metal screen or fabric, and water is pumped through the layer. Pressure filters and diatomaceous earth filters are used most often for industrial applications or for public swimming pools.

Microstrainers consist of a finely woven stainless-steel wire cloth mounted on a revolving drum that is partially submerged in the water. Water enters through an open end of the drum and flows out through the screen, leaving suspended solids behind. Captured solids are washed into a hopper when they are carried up out of the water by the rotating drum. Microstrainers are used mainly to remove algae from surface water supplies before conventional gravity-flow filtration. (They can also be employed in advanced wastewater treatment.)

DISINFECTION

Disinfection destroys pathogenic bacteria and is essential to prevent the spread of waterborne disease. Typically the final process in drinking-water treatment, it is accomplished by applying either chlorine or chlorine compounds, ozone, or ultraviolet radiation to clarified water.

The addition of chlorine or chlorine compounds to drinking water is called chlorination. Chlorine compounds may be applied in liquid or solid forms; for instance, liquid sodium hypochlorite or calcium hypochlorite in tablet or ganular form. However, the direct application of gaseous chlorine from pressurized steel containers is usually the most economical method for disinfecting large volumes of water.

Taste or ordour problems are minimized with proper dosages of chlorine at the treatment plant. A residual concentration can be maintained throughout the distribution system to ensure a safe level at points of use. Chlorine can combine eith certina naturally occurring organic compounds in water to produce chloroform and other potentially harmful by-products (trihalomethanes). The risk of this is small, however, when chlorine is applied after coagulation, sedimentation, and filtration.

The use of chemical compounds called chloramines (chlorine combined with ammonia) for disinfecting public water supplies has been increasing since the beginning of the 21st century. This disinfection method is often called chloramination. The disinfecting effect of chloramines lasts longer than that of chlorine alone, further protecting water quality throughout the distribution system. Also, chloramines further reduce taste and odour problems, and produce lower levels of harmful by-products, compared with the use of chlorine alone.

Ozone gas may be used for disinfection of drinking water. However, since ozone is unstable, it cannot be stored and must be produced on-site, making the process more expensive than chlorination. Ozone has the advantage of not causing taste or odour problems; it leaves no residual in the disinfected water. The lack of an ozone residual, however, makes it difficult to monitor its continued effectiveness as water flows through the distribution system.

Ultraviolet radiation destroys pathogens, and its use as a disinfecting agent eliminates the need to handle chemicals. It leaves no residual, and it does not cause taste or odour problems. But the high cost of its application makes it a poor competitor with either chlorine or ozone as a disinfectant.

ADDITIONAL TREATMENT

Clarification and disinfection are the conventional processes for purifying surface water supplies. Other techniques may be used in addition, or separately, to remove certain impurities, depending on the quality of the raw water.

MEMBRANE FILTRATION

Several types of synthetic semipermeable membranes can be used to block the flow of particles and molecules while allowing smaller water molecules to pass through under the effect of hydrostatic pressure. Pressure-driven membrane filtration systems include microfiltration (MF), ultrafiltration (UF), and reverse osmosis (RO); they differ basically in the pressures used and pore sizes of the membranes. RO systems operate at relatively high pressures and can be used to remove dissolved inorganic compounds from water. Both MF and UF systems operate under lower pressures and are typically used for the removal of particles and microbes. They can provide increased assurances of safe drinking water because the microbial contaminants (viruses, bacteria, and protozoa) can be completely removed by a physical barrier. Low-pressure membrane filtration of public water supplies has increased significantly since the late 1990s because of improvements in membrane manufacturing technology and decreases in cost.

WATER SOFTENING

Softening is the process of removing the dissolved calcium and magnesium salts that cause hardness in water. It is achieved either by adding chemicals that form insoluble precipitates or by ion exchange. Chemicals used for softening include calcium hydroxide (slaked lime) and sodium carbonate (soda ash). The lime-soda method of water softening must be followed by sedimentation and filtration in order to remove the precipitates. Ion exchange is accomplished by passing the water through columns of a natural or synthetic resin that trades sodium ions for calcium and magnesium ions. Ion-exchange columns must eventually be regenerated by washing with a sodium chloride solution.

AERATION

Aeration is a physical treatment process used for taste and odour control and for removal of dissolved iron and manganese. It consists of spraying water into the air or cascading it downward through stacks of perforated trays. Dissolved gases that cause tastes and odours are transferred from the water to the air. Oxygen from the air, meanwhile, reacts with any iron and manganese in the water, forming a precipitate that is removed by sedimentation and filtration.

Carbon Adsorption

An effective method for removing dissolved organic substances that cause tastes, odours, or colours is adsorption by activated carbon. Adsorption is the capacity of a solid particle to attract molecules to its surface. Powdered carbon mixed with water can adsorb and hold many different organic impurities. When the carbon is saturated with impurities, it is cleaned or reactivated by heating to a high temperature in a special furnace.

Fluoridation

Many communities reduce the incidence of tooth decay in young children by adding sodium fluoride or other fluorine compounds to filtered water. The dosage of fluoride must be carefully controlled. Low concentrations are beneficial and cause no harmful side effects, but very high concentrations of fluoride may cause discoloration of tooth enamel.

DESALINATION

Desalination, or desalting, is the separation of fresh water from salt water or brackish water. Major advances in desalination technology have taken place since the 1950s, as the need for supplies of fresh water has grown in arid and densely populated areas of the world. Desalted water is the main source of municipal supply in areas of the Caribbean, the Middle East, and North Africa, and its use is increasing in the southeastern United States. Although it is relatively expensive to produce, desalted water can be more economical than the alternative of transporting large quantities of fresh water over long distances.

There are two basic types of desalting techniques: thermal processes and membrane processes. Both types consume considerable amounts of energy. Thermal methods involve heat transfer and a phase change of the water from liquid into vapour or ice. Membrane methods use very thin sheets of special plastic that act as selective barriers, allowing pure water to be separated from the salt.

THERMAL PROCESSES

Distillation, a thermal process that includes heating, evaporation, and condensation, is the oldest and most widely used of desalination technologies. Modern methods for the distillation of large quantities of salt water rely on the fact that the boiling temperature of water is lowered as air pressure drops, significantly reducing the amount of energy needed to vaporize the water. Systems that utilize this principle include multistage flash distillation, multiple-effect distillation, and vapour-compression distillation.

Multistage flash distillation plants account for more than half of the world production of desalted water. The process is carried out in a series of closed vessels (stages) set at progressively lower internal pressures. Heat is added to the system from a boiler. When preheated salt water enters a low-pressure chamber, some of it rapidly boils, or flashes, into water vapour. The vapour is condensed into fresh water on heat-exchange tubes that run through each stage. These tubes carry incoming seawater, thereby reducing the heat required from the boiler. Fresh water collects in trays under the tubes. The remaining brine flows into the next stage at even lower pressure, where some of it again flashes into vapour. A multistage flash plant may have as many as 40 stages, permitting salt water to boil repeatedly without supplying additional heat.

Multiple-effect distillation also takes place in a series of low-pressure vessels (effects), but it differs from multistage distillation in that preheated salt water is sprayed onto evaporator tubes in order to promote rapid evaporation in each vessel. This process requires pumping the salt water from one effect to the next.

In the vapour-compression system, heat is provided by the compression of vapour rather than by direct heat input from a boiler. When the vapour is rapidly compressed, its temperature rises. Some of the compressed and heated vapour is then recycled through a series of tubes passing through a reduced-pressure chamber, where evaporation of salt water occurs. Electricity is the main source of energy for this process. It is used for small-scale desalting applications—for example, at coastal resorts.

Another thermal process is solar humidification. Salt water is collected in shallow basins in a "still," a structure similar to a greenhouse. The water is warmed as sunlight enters through inclined glass or plastic covers. Water vapour rises, condenses on the cooler covers, and trickles down to a collecting trough. Thermal energy from the sun is free, but a solar still is expensive to build, requires a large land area, and needs additional energy for pumping water to and from the facility. Solar humidification units are suitable for providing desalted water to individual families or for very small villages where sunlight is abundant.

The freezing process of desalination, also called crystallization, involves cooling salt water to form crystals of pure ice. The ice crystals are separated from the unfrozen brine, rinsed to remove residual salt, and then melted to produce fresh water. Freezing is theoretically more efficient than distillation, and scaling as well as corrosion problems are lessened at the lower operating temperatures, but the mechanical difficulties of handling mixtures of ice and water prevent the construction of large-scale commercial plants. In hot climates, heat leakage into the facility is also a significant problem.

MEMBRANE PROCESSES

Two commercially important membrane processes used for desalination are electrodialysis and reverse osmosis. They are used mainly to desalt brackish or highly mineralized water supplies rather than much saltier seawater. In both methods, thin plastic sheets act as selective barriers, allowing fresh water but not salt to flow through.

Most salts dissolved in water exist in the form of electrically charged particles called ions. Half are positively charged (e.g., sodium), and half are negatively charged (e.g., chloride). In electrodialysis an electric voltage is applied across the saline solution. This causes ions to migrate toward the electrode that has a charge opposite to that of their own. In a typical electrodialysis unit, several hundred plastic membranes that are selectively permeable to either positive ions or negative ions, but not both, are closely spaced in alternation and bound together with electrodes on the outside. Incoming salt water flows between the membrane sheets. Under the applied voltage the ions move in opposite directions through the membranes, but they are trapped by the next membrane in the stack. This forms alternate cells of dilute salt water and brine. The more-dilute solution is recycled back through the stack until it reaches freshwater quality.

When a semipermeable membrane separates two solutions of different concentrations, there is a natural tendency for the concentrations to become equalized. Water flows from the dilute side to the concentrated side.

This process is called osmosis. However, a high pressure applied to the concentrated side can reverse the direction of this flow. In reverse osmosis, salty water is pumped into a vessel and pressurized against the membrane. Fresh water diffuses through the membrane, leaving a more concentrated salt solution behind.

Next to multistage flash distillation, reverse osmosis is the second-ranking desalting process. It will play a greater role in the desalting of seawater and brackish water as more-durable membranes are developed. It can also be applied to the advanced treatment of municipal sewage and industrial wastewater.

Cogeneration and Hybrid Processes

Desalting costs are reduced by using cogeneration and hybrid processes. Cogeneration (or dual-purpose) desalination plants are large-scale facilities that produce both electric power and desalted seawater. Distillation methods in particular are suitable for cogeneration. The high-pressure steam that runs electric generators can be recycled in the distillation unit's brine heater. This significantly reduces fuel consumption compared with what is required if separate facilities are built. Cogeneration is very common in the Middle East and North Africa.

Hybrid systems are units that operate with two or more different desalting processes (e.g., distillation and reverse osmosis). They offer further economic benefits when employed in cogeneration plants, productively combining the operation of each process.

Effluent Disposal

Desalination produces not only fresh water, but also a significant volume of waste effluent, called brine. Since the primary pollutant in the brine is salt, disposal in the ocean is generally not a problem for facilities located near a coastline. At inland desalination facilities, care must be taken to prevent pollution of groundwater or surface waters. Methods of brine disposal include dilution, evaporation, injection into a saline aquifer, and pipeline transport to a suitable disposal point.

SEWAGE TREATMENT

Sewage treatment (also called wastewater treatment) is the removal of impurities from sewage, or wastewater, before they reach aquifers or natural bodies of water such as rivers, lakes, estuaries, and oceans. Water pollution is caused primarily by the drainage of contaminated wastewater into surface water or groundwater, and therefore sewage treatment is a major element of water pollution control.

HISTORICAL BACKGROUND

Many ancient cities had drainage systems, but they were primarily intended to carry rainwater away from roofs and pavements. A notable example is the drainage system of ancient Rome. It included many surface conduits that were connected to a large vaulted channel called the Cloaca Maxima ("Great Sewer"), which carried drainage water to the Tiber River. Built of stone and on a grand scale, the Cloaca Maxima is one of the oldest existing monuments of Roman engineering.

There was little progress in urban drainage or sewerage during the Middle Ages. Privy vaults and cesspools were used, but most wastes were simply dumped into gutters to be flushed through the drains by floods. Toilets (water closets) were installed in houses in the early 19th

A worker in Rome inspects passages of the ancient Cloaca Maxima, or "Great Sewer," which once emptied sewage into the Tiber River. Stephen L. Alvarez/ National Geographic/Getty Images

century, but they were usually connected to cesspools, not to sewers. In densely populated areas, local conditions soon became intolerable because the cesspools were seldom emptied and frequently overflowed. The threat to public health became apparent. In England in the middle of the 19th century, outbreaks of cholera were traced directly to well-water supplies contaminated with human waste from privy vaults and cesspools. It soon became necessary for all water closets in the larger towns to be connected directly to the storm sewers. This transferred sewage from the ground near houses to nearby bodies of water. Thus, a new problem emerged—surface water pollution.

It used to be said that "the solution to pollution is dilution." When small amounts of sewage are discharged into a flowing body of water, a natural process of stream self-purification occurs. Densely populated communities generate such large quantities of sewage, however, that dilution alone does not prevent pollution. This makes it necessary to treat or purify wastewater to some degree before disposal.

The construction of centralized sewage treatment plants began in the late 19th and early 20th centuries, principally in the United Kingdom and the United States. Instead of discharging sewage directly into a nearby body of water, it was first passed through a combination of physical, biological, and chemical processes that removed some or most of the pollutants. Also beginning in the 1900s, new sewage-collection systems were designed to separate storm water from domestic wastewater, so that treatment plants did not become overloaded during periods of wet weather.

After the middle of the 20th century, increasing public concern for environmental quality led to broader and more stringent regulation of wastewater disposal practices. Higher levels of treatment were required. For example, pretreatment of industrial wastewater, with the aim of preventing toxic chemicals from interfering with the biological processes used at sewage treatment plants, often became a necessity. In fact, wastewater treatment technology advanced to the point where it became possible to remove virtually all pollutants from sewage. This was so expensive, however, that such high levels of treatment were not usually justified.

Wastewater treatment plants became large, complex facilities that required considerable amounts of energy for their operation. After the rise of oil prices in the 1970s, concern for energy conservation became a more important factor in the design of new pollution control systems. Consequently, land disposal and subsurface disposal of sewage began to receive increased attention where feasible. Such "low-tech" pollution control methods not only might help to conserve energy but also might serve to recycle nutrients and replenish groundwater supplies.

SEWAGE CHARACTERISTICS

There are three types of sewage: domestic sewage, industrial sewage, and storm sewage. Domestic sewage carries used water from houses and apartments; it is also called sanitary sewage. Industrial sewage is used water from manufacturing or chemical processes. Storm sewage, or storm water, is runoff from precipitation that is collected in a system of pipes or open channels.

Domestic sewage is slightly more than 99.9 percent pure water by weight. The rest, less than 0.1 percent, contains a wide variety of dissolved and suspended impurities. Although amounting to a very small fraction of the sewage by weight, the nature of these impurities and the large volumes of sewage in which they are carried make disposal of domestic wastewater a significant technical problem. The principal impurities are putrescible organic materials and plant nutrients, but domestic sewage is also very likely to contain disease-causing microbes. Industrial wastewater usually contains specific and readily identifiable chemical compounds, depending on the nature of the industrial process. Storm sewage carries organic materials, suspended and dissolved solids, and other substances picked up as it travels over the ground.

ORGANIC MATERIAL

The amount of putrescible organic material in sewage is measured by the biochemical oxygen demand, or BOD. In other words, BOD is the amount of oxygen required by microorganisms to decompose the organic substances in sewage. The more organic material there is in the sewage, the higher the BOD. BOD is among the most important parameters for the design and operation of sewage treatment plants. Industrial sewage may have BOD levels many times that of domestic sewage. The BOD of storm sewage is of particular concern when it is mixed with domestic sewage in combined sewerage systems.

Dissolved oxygen is an important water quality factor for lakes and rivers. The higher the concentration of dissolved oxygen, the better the water quality. When sewage enters a lake or stream, decomposition of the organic materials begins. Oxygen is consumed as microorganisms use it in their metabolism. This can quickly deplete the available oxygen in the water. When the dissolved oxygen levels drop too low, trout and other aquatic species soon perish. In fact, if the oxygen level drops to zero, the water will become septic. Decomposition of organic compounds without oxygen causes the undesirable odours usually associated with septic or putrid conditions.

Suspended Solids

Another important characteristic of sewage is suspended solids. The volume of sludge produced in a treatment plant is directly related to the total suspended solids present in the sewage. Industrial and storm sewage may contain higher concentrations of suspended solids than domestic sewage. The extent to which a treatment plant removes suspended solids, as well as BOD, determines the efficiency of the treatment process.

Plant Nutrients and Microbes

Domestic sewage contains compounds of nitrogen and phosphorus, two elements that are basic nutrients essential for the growth of plants. In lakes, excessive amounts of nitrates and phosphates can cause the rapid growth of algae. Algal blooms, often caused by sewage discharges, accelerate the natural aging of lakes in a process called eutrophication.

Domestic sewage contains many millions of microorganisms per gallon. Most are coliform bacteria from the human intestinal tract, and domestic sewage is also likely to carry other microbes. Coliforms are used as indicators of sewage pollution. A high coliform count usually indicates recent sewage pollution.

SEWERAGE SYSTEMS

A sewerage system, or wastewater collection system, is a network of pipes, pumping stations, and appurtenances that convey sewage from its points of origin to a point of treatment and disposal.

COMBINED SYSTEMS

Systems that carry a mixture of both domestic sewage and storm sewage are called combined sewers. Combined sewers typically consist of large-diameter pipes or tunnels, because of the large volumes of storm water that must be carried during wet-weather periods. They are very common in older cities but are no longer designed and built as part of new sewerage facilities. Because wastewater treatment plants cannot handle large volumes of storm water, sewage must bypass the treatment plants during wet weather and be discharged directly into the receiving water. These combined sewer overflows, containing untreated domestic sewage, cause recurring water pollution problems and are very troublesome sources of pollution.

In some large cities the combined sewer overflow problem has been reduced by diverting the first flush of combined sewage into a large basin or underground tunnel. After temporary storage, it can be treated by settling and disinfection before being discharged into a receiving body of water, or it can be treated in a nearby wastewater treatment plant at a rate that will not overload the facility. Another method for controlling combined sewage involves the use of swirl concentrators. These direct sewage through cylindrically shaped devices that create a vortex, or whirlpool, effect. The vortex helps concentrate impurities in a much smaller volume of water for treatment.

SEPARATE SYSTEMS

New wastewater collection facilities are designed as separate systems, carrying either domestic sewage or storm sewage but not both. Storm sewers usually carry surface runoff to a point of disposal in a stream or river. Small detention basins may be built as part of the system, storing storm water temporarily and reducing the magnitude of the peak flow rate. Sanitary sewers, on the other hand, carry domestic wastewater to a sewage treatment plant. Pretreated industrial wastewater may be allowed into municipal sanitary sewerage systems, but storm water is excluded.

Storm sewers are usually built with sections of reinforced concrete pipe. Corrugated metal pipes may be used in some cases. Storm water inlets or catch basins are located at suitable intervals in a street right-of-way or in easements across private property. The pipelines are usually located to allow downhill gravity flow to a nearby stream or to a detention basin. Storm water pumping stations are avoided, if possible, because of the very large pump capacities that would be needed to handle the intermittent flows.

A sanitary sewerage system includes laterals, submains, and interceptors. Except for individual house connections, laterals are the smallest sewers in the network. They usually are not less than 200 mm (8 inches) in diameter and carry sewage by gravity into larger submains, or collector sewers. The collector sewers tie in to a main interceptor, or trunk line, which carries the sewage to a treatment plant. Interceptors are usually built with precast sections of reinforced concrete pipe, up to 5 metres (15 ft) in diameter. Other materials used for sanitary sewers include vitrified clay, asbestos cement, plastic, steel, or ductile iron. The use of plastic for laterals is increasing because of its lightness and ease of installation. Iron and steel pipes are used for force mains or in pumping stations. Force mains are pipelines that carry sewage under pressure when it must be pumped.

ALTERNATIVE SYSTEMS

Sometimes the cost of conventional gravity sewers can be prohibitively high because of low population densities or site conditions such as a high water table or bedrock. Three alternative wastewater collection systems that may be used under these circumstances include small-diameter gravity sewers, pressure sewers, and vacuum sewers.

In small-diameter gravity systems, septic tanks are first used to remove settleable and floating solids from the wastewater from each house before it flows into a network of collector mains (typically 100 mm, or 4 inches, in diameter); these systems are most suitable for small rural communities. Because they do not carry grease, grit and sewage solids, the pipes can be of smaller diameter and placed at reduced slopes or gradients to minimize trench excavation costs. Pressure sewers are best used in flat areas or where expensive rock excavation would be required. Grinder pumps discharge wastewater from each home into the main pressure sewer, which can follow the slope of the ground. In a vacuum sewerage system, sewage from one or more buildings flows by gravity into a sump or tank from which it is pulled out by vacuum pumps located at a central vacuum station and then flows into a collection tank. From the vacuum collection tank the sewage is pumped to a treatment plant.

PUMPS

Pumping stations are built when sewage must be raised from a low point to a point of higher elevation or where the topography prevents downhill gravity flow. Special nonclogging pumps are available to handle raw sewage. They are installed in structures called lift stations. There are two basic types of lift stations: dry well and wet well. A wet-well installation has only one chamber or tank to receive and hold the sewage until it is pumped out. Specially designed submersible pumps and motors can be located at the bottom of the chamber, completely below the water level. Dry-well installations have two separate chambers, one to receive the wastewater and one to enclose and protect the pumps and controls. The protective dry chamber allows easy access for inspection and maintenance. All sewage lift stations, whether of the wet-well or dry-well type, should include at least two pumps. One pump can operate while the other is removed for repair.

FLOW RATES

There is a wide variation in sewage flow rates over the course of a day. A sewerage system must accommodate this variation. In most cities domestic sewage flow rates are highest in the morning and evening hours. They are lowest during the middle of the night. Flow quantities depend upon population density, water consumption, and the extent of commercial or industrial activity in the community. The average sewage flow rate is usually about the same as the average water use in the community. In a lateral sewer, short-term peak flow rates can be roughly four times the average flow rate. In a trunk sewer, peak flow rates may be two-and-a-half times the average.

Sewage Treatment and Disposal

The predominant method of sewage disposal in large cities and towns is discharge into a body of surface water. Suburban and rural areas rely more on subsurface disposal. In either case, sewage must be purified or treated to some degree in order to protect both public health and water quality. Suspended particulates and biodegradable organics must be removed to varying extents. Pathogenic bacteria must be destroyed. It may also be necessary to remove nitrates and phosphates (plant nutrients) and to neutralize or remove industrial wastes and toxic chemicals.

The degree to which sewage must be treated varies, depending on local environmental conditions and governmental standards. Two pertinent types of standards are stream standards and effluent standards. Stream standards, designed to prevent the deterioration of existing water quality, set limits on the amounts of specific pollutants allowed in streams, rivers, and lakes. The limits depend on a classification of the "maximum beneficial use" of the water. Water quality parameters that are regulated by stream standards include dissolved oxygen, coliforms, turbidity, acidity, and toxic substances. Effluent standards, on the other hand, pertain directly to the quality of the treated sewage discharged from a sewage treatment plant. The factors controlled under these standards usually include biochemical oxygen demand (BOD), suspended solids, acidity, and coliforms.

There are three levels of sewage treatment: primary, secondary, and tertiary (or advanced). Primary treatment removes about 60 percent of total suspended solids and about 35 percent of BOD; dissolved impurities are not removed. It is usually used as a first step before secondary treatment. Secondary treatment removes more than 85 percent of both suspended solids and BOD. A minimum level of secondary treatment is usually required in the United States and other developed countries. When more than 85 percent of total solids and BOD must be removed, or when dissolved nitrate and phosphate levels must be reduced, tertiary treatment methods are used. Tertiary processes can remove more than 99 percent of all the impurities from sewage, producing an effluent of almost drinking-water quality. Tertiary treatment can be very expensive, often doubling the cost of secondary treatment. It is used only under special circumstances.

For all levels of sewage treatment, the last step prior to discharge of the sewage effluent into a body of surface water is disinfection. Disinfection is usually accomplished by mixing the effluent with chlorine gas in a contact tank for at least 15 minutes. Because chlorine residuals in the effluent may have adverse effects on aquatic life, an additional chemical may be added to dechlorinate the effluent. Ultraviolet radiation, which can disinfect without leaving any residual in the effluent, is becoming more competitive with chlorine as a sewage disinfectant.

PRIMARY TREATMENT

Primary treatment removes material that will either float or readily settle out by gravity. It includes the physical processes of screening, comminution, grit removal, and sedimentation. Screens are made of long, closely spaced, narrow metal bars. They block floating debris such as wood, rags, and other bulky objects that could clog pipes or pumps. In modern plants the screens are cleaned mechanically, and the material is promptly disposed of by burial on the plant grounds. A comminutor may be used to grind and shred debris that passes through the screens. The shredded material is removed later by sedimentation or flotation processes.

Grit chambers are long narrow tanks that are designed to slow down the flow so that solids such as sand, coffee grounds, and eggshells will settle out of the water. Grit causes excessive wear and tear on pumps and other plant equipment. Its removal is particularly important in cities with combined sewer systems, which carry a good deal of silt, sand, and gravel that wash off streets or land during a storm.

Suspended solids that pass through screens and grit chambers are removed from the sewage in sedimentation tanks. These tanks, also called primary clarifiers, provide about two hours of detention time for gravity settling to take place. As the sewage flows through them slowly, the solids gradually sink to the bottom. The settled solids— known as raw or primary sludge—are moved along the tank bottom by mechanical scrapers. Sludge is collected in a hopper, where it is pumped out for removal. Mechanical surface-skimming devices remove grease and other floating materials.

SECONDARY TREATMENT

Secondary treatment removes the soluble organic matter that escapes primary treatment. It also removes more of the suspended solids. Removal is usually accomplished by biological processes in which microbes consume the organic impurities as food, converting them into carbon dioxide, water, and energy for their own growth and reproduction. The sewage treatment plant provides a suitable environment, albeit of steel and concrete, for this natural biological process. Removal of soluble organic matter at the treatment plant helps to protect the dissolved oxygen balance of a receiving stream, river, or lake.

There are three basic biological treatment methods: the trickling filter, the activated sludge process, and the oxidation pond. A fourth, less common method is the rotating biological contacter.

Trickling Filter

A trickling filter is simply a tank filled with a deep bed of stones. Settled sewage is sprayed continuously over the top of the stones and trickles to the bottom, where it is collected for further treatment. As the sewage trickles down, bacteria gather and multiply on the stones. The steady flow of sewage over these growths allows the microbes to absorb the dissolved organics, thus lowering the BOD of the sewage. Air circulating upward through the spaces among the stones provides sufficient oxygen for the metabolic processes.

Settling tanks, called secondary clarifiers, follow the trickling filters. These clarifiers remove microbes that are washed off the rocks by the flow of sewage. Two or more trickling filters may be connected in series, and sewage can be recirculated in order to increase treatment efficiencies.

Activated Sludge

The activated sludge treatment system consists of an aeration tank followed by a secondary clarifier. Settled sewage, mixed with fresh sludge that is recirculated from the secondary clarifier, is introduced into the aeration tank. Compressed air is then injected into the mixture through porous diffusers located at the bottom of the tank. As it bubbles to the surface, the diffused air provides oxygen and a rapid mixing action. Air can also be added by the

Aeration tanks (foreground) bubble compressed air through a mixture of fresh sewage and recirculated sludge. The aeration and mixing action activate bacteria that digest organic matter in the sewage. © www.istockphoto.com/ ymgerman

churning action of mechanical propeller-like mixers located at the tank surface.

Under such oxygenated conditions, microorganisms thrive, forming an active, healthy suspension of biological solids—mostly bacteria—called activated sludge. About six hours of detention is provided in the aeration tank. This gives the microbes enough time to absorb dissolved organics from the sewage, reducing the BOD. The mixture then flows from the aeration tank into the secondary clarifier, where activated sludge settles out by gravity. Clear water is skimmed from the surface of the clarifier, disinfected, and discharged as secondary effluent. The sludge is pumped out from a hopper at the bottom of the tank. About 30 percent of the sludge is recirculated back into the aeration tank, where it is mixed with the primary effluent. This recirculation is a key feature of the activated sludge process. The recycled microbes are well acclimated to the sewage environment and readily metabolize the organic materials in the primary effluent. The remaining 70 percent of the secondary sludge must be treated and disposed of in an acceptable manner.

Variations of the activated sludge process include extended aeration, contact stabilization, and high-purity oxygen aeration. Extended aeration and contact stabilization systems omit the primary settling step. They are efficient for treating small sewage flows from motels, schools, and other relatively isolated sewage sources. Both of these treatments are usually provided in prefabricated steel tanks called package plants. Oxygen aeration systems mix pure oxygen with activated sludge. A richer concentration of oxygen allows the aeration time to be shortened from six to two hours, reducing the required tank volume.

Oxidation Pond

Oxidation ponds, also called lagoons or stabilization ponds, are large, shallow ponds designed to treat sewage through the interaction of sunlight, bacteria, and algae. Algae grow using energy from the sun and carbon dioxide and inorganic compounds released by bacteria in water. During the process of photosynthesis, the algae release oxygen needed by aerobic bacteria. Mechanical aerators are sometimes installed to supply yet more oxygen, thereby reducing the required size of the pond. Sludge deposits in the pond must eventually be removed by dredging. Algae remaining in the pond effluent can be removed by filtration or by a combination of chemical treatment and settling.

Rotating Biological Contacter

In this treatment system a series of large plastic disks mounted on a horizontal shaft are partially submerged in primary effluent. As the shaft rotates, the disks are exposed alternately to air and sewage, allowing a layer of bacteria to grow on the disks and to metabolize the organics in the sewage.

TERTIARY TREATMENT

When the intended receiving water is very vulnerable to the effects of pollution, secondary effluent may be treated further by several tertiary processes. These include effluent polishing, the removal of plant nutrients, and land treatments. New treatments—such as membrane bioreactor process, the ballasted floc reactor, and the integrated fixed-film activated sludge process—have been added to many older sewage treatment facilities as precautionary treatments to ensure high water quality.

Effluent Polishing

For the removal of additional suspended solids and BOD from secondary effluent, effluent polishing is an effective treatment. It is most often accomplished using granular media filters, much like the filters used to purify drinking water. Polishing filters are usually built as prefabricated units, with tanks placed directly above the filters for storing backwash water. Effluent polishing of sewage may also be achieved using microstrainers of the type used in treating municipal water supplies.

Removal of Plant Nutrients

When treatment standards require the removal of plant nutrients from the sewage, it is often done as a tertiary step. Phosphorus in sewage is usually present in the form of organic compounds and phosphates that can easily be removed by chemical precipitation. This process, however, increases the volume and weight of sludge. Nitrogen, another important plant nutrient, is present in sewage in the form of ammonia and nitrates. Ammonia is toxic to fish, and it also exerts an oxygen demand in receiving waters as it is converted to nitrates. Nitrates, like phosphates, promote the growth of algae and the eutrophication of lakes. A method called nitrification-denitrification can be used to remove the nitrates. It is a two-step biological process in which ammonia nitrogen is first converted into nitrates by microorganisms. The nitrates are further metabolized by another species of bacteria, forming nitrogen gas that escapes into the air. This process requires the construction of more aeration and settling tanks and significantly increases the cost of treatment.

A physicochemical process called ammonia stripping may be used to remove ammonia from sewage. Chemicals are added to convert ammonium ions into ammonia gas. The sewage is then cascaded down through a tower, allowing the gas to come out of solution and escape into the air. Stripping is less expensive than nitrification-denitrification, but it does not work very efficiently in cold weather.

Land Treatment

In some locations, secondary effluent can be applied directly to the ground and a polished effluent obtained by natural processes as the sewage flows over vegetation and percolates through the soil. There are three types of land treatment: slow-rate, rapid infiltration, and overland flow.

In the slow-rate, or irrigation, method, effluent is applied onto the land by ridge-and-furrow spreading (in ditches) or by sprinkler systems. Most of the water and nutrients are absorbed by the roots of growing vegetation. In the rapid infiltration method, the sewage is stored in large ponds called recharge basins. Most of it percolates to the groundwater, and very little is absorbed by vegetation. For this method to work, soils must be highly permeable. In overland flow, sewage is sprayed onto an inclined vegetated terrace and slowly flows to a collection ditch. Purification is achieved by physical, chemical, and biological processes, and the collected water is usually discharged into a nearby stream.

Land treatment of sewage can provide moisture and nutrients for the growth of vegetation, such as corn or grain for animal feed. It also can recharge, or replenish, groundwater aquifers. Land treatment, in effect, allows sewage to be recycled for beneficial use. Large land areas are required, however, and the feasibility of this kind of treatment may be limited further by soil texture and climate.

New Treatment Technologies

Many older sewage treatment facilities require upgrading due to increasingly strict water quality standards, but this is often difficult because of limited space for expansion. In order to allow improvement of treatment efficiencies without requiring more land area, new treatment methods have been developed. These include the membrane bioreactor process, the ballasted floc reactor, and the integrated fixed-film activated sludge process.

In the membrane bioreactor process, hollow-fibre microfiltration membrane modules are submerged in a single tank in which aeration, secondary clarification, and filtration can occur, thereby providing both secondary and tertiary treatment in a small land area. In a ballasted floc reactor, the settling rate of suspended solids is increased by using sand and a polymer to help coagulate the suspended solids and form larger masses called flocs. The sand is separated from the sludge in a hydroclone, a relatively simple apparatus into which the water is introduced near the top of a cylinder at a tangent so that heavy materials such as sand are "spun" by centrifugal force toward the outside wall. The sand collects by gravity at the bottom of the hydroclone and is recycled back to the reactor. Biological aerated filters use a basin with submerged media that serves as both a contact surface for biological treatment and a filter to separate solids from the wastewater. Fine-bubble aeration is applied to facilitate the process, and routine backwashing is used to clean the media. The land area required for a biological aerated filter is only about 15 percent of the area required for a conventional activated sludge system.

ON-SITE SEPTIC TANKS AND LEACHING FIELDS

In sparsely populated suburban or rural areas, it is usually not economical to build sewage collection systems and a centrally located treatment plant. Instead, a separate treatment and disposal system is provided for each home. On-site systems provide effective, low-cost, long-term solutions for sewage disposal as long as they are properly designed, installed, and maintained. In the United States, about one-third of private homes make use of an on-site subsurface disposal system.

The most common type of on-site system includes a buried, watertight septic tank and a subsurface absorption field (also called a drain field or leaching field). The septic tank serves as a primary sedimentation and sludge storage chamber, removing most of the settleable and floating material from the influent sewage. Although the sludge decomposes anaerobically, it eventually accumulates at the tank bottom and must be pumped out periodically (every 2 to 4 years). Floating solids and grease are trapped by a baffle at the tank outlet, and settled sewage flows out into the absorption field, through which it percolates downward into the ground. As it flows slowly through layers of soil, the settled sewage is further treated and purified by both physical and biological processes before it reaches the water table.

An absorption field includes several perforated pipelines placed in long, shallow trenches filled with gravel. The

The components of a septic tank being installed in a homeowner's yard. Septic tanks are individual sewage treatment and disposal units, frequently used in areas where sewerage systems have not been installed.. Shutterstock.com

pipes distribute the effluent over a sizable area as it seeps through the gravel and into the underlying layers of soil. If the disposal site is too small for a conventional leaching field, deeper seepage pits may be used instead of shallow trenches; seepage pits require less land area than leaching fields. Both leaching field trenches and seepage pits must be placed above seasonally high groundwater levels.

For subsurface on-site sewage disposal to succeed, the permeability, or hydraulic conductivity, of the soil must be within an acceptable range. If it is too low, the effluent will not be able to flow effectively through the soil, and it may seep out onto the surface of the absorption field, thereby endangering public health. If permeability is too high, there may not be sufficient purification before the effluent reaches the water table, thereby contaminating the groundwater. The capacity of the ground to absorb settled sewage depends largely on the texture of the soil (i.e., relative amounts of gravel, sand, silt, and clay). Permeability can be evaluated by direct observation of the soil in excavated test pits and also by conducting a percolation test, or "perc test." The perc test measures the rate at which water seeps into the soil in small test holes dug on the disposal site. The measured perc rate can be used to determine the total required area of the absorption field or the number of seepage pits.

Where unfavourable site or soil conditions prohibit the use of both absorption fields and seepage pits, mound systems may be utilized for on-site sewage disposal. A mound is an absorption field built above the natural ground surface in order to provide suitable material for percolation and to separate the drain field from the water table. Septic tank effluent is intermittently pumped from a chamber and applied to the mound. Other alternative on-site disposal methods include use of intermittent sand filters or of small, prefabricated aerobic treatment units. Disinfection (usually by chlorination) of the effluent from these systems is required when the effluent is discharged into a nearby stream.

WASTEWATER REUSE

Wastewater can be a valuable resource in cities or towns where population is growing and water supplies are limited. In addition to easing the strain on limited freshwater supplies, the reuse of wastewater can improve the quality of streams and lakes by reducing the effluent discharges that they receive. Wastewater may be reclaimed and reused for crop and landscape irrigation, groundwater recharge, or recreational purposes. Reclamation for drinking is technically possible, but this reuse faces significant public resistance.

There are two types of wastewater reuse: direct and indirect. In direct reuse, treated wastewater is piped into some type of water system without first being diluted in a natural stream or lake or in groundwater. One example is the irrigation of a golf course with effluent from a municipal wastewater treatment plant. Indirect reuse involves the mixing of reclaimed wastewater with another body of water before reuse. In effect, any community that uses a surface water supply downstream from the treatment plant discharge pipe of another community is indirectly reusing wastewater. Indirect reuse is also accomplished by discharging reclaimed wastewater into a groundwater aquifer and later withdrawing the water for use. Discharge into an aquifer (called artificial recharge) is done by either deep-well injection or shallow surface spreading.

Quality and treatment requirements for reclaimed wastewater become more stringent as the chances for direct human contact and ingestion increase. The impurities that must be removed depend on the intended use of the water. For example, removal of phosphates or nitrates is not necessary if the intended use is landscape irrigation. If direct reuse as a potable supply is intended, tertiary treatment with multiple barriers against contaminants is required. This may include secondary treatment followed by granular media filtration, ultraviolet radiation, granular activated carbon adsorption, reverse osmosis, air stripping, ozonation, and chlorination.

The use of gray-water recycling systems in new commercial buildings offers a method of saving water and reducing total sewage volumes. These systems filter and chlorinate drainage from tubs and sinks and reuse the water for nonpotable purposes (e.g., flushing toilets and urinals). Recycled water can be marked with a blue dye to ensure that it is not used for potable purposes.

Sludge Treatment and Disposal

The residue that accumulates in sewage treatment plants is called sludge (or biosolids). Treatment and disposal of sewage sludge are major factors in the design and operation of all wastewater treatment plants. Two basic goals of treating sludge before final disposal are to reduce its volume and to stabilize the organic materials. Stabilized sludge does not have an offensive odour and can be handled without causing a nuisance or health hazard. Smaller sludge volume reduces the costs of pumping and storage.

SLUDGE TREATMENT METHODS

Treatment of sewage sludge may include a combination of thickening, digestion, and dewatering processes.

Thickening

Thickening is usually the first step in sludge treatment because it is impractical to handle thin sludge, a slurry of solids suspended in water. Thickening is usually accomplished in a tank called a gravity thickener. A thickener can reduce the total volume of sludge to less than half the original volume. An alternative to gravity thickening is dissolved-air flotation. In this method, air bubbles carry the solids to the surface, where a layer of thickened sludge forms.

Digestion

Sludge digestion is a biological process in which organic solids are decomposed into stable substances. Digestion reduces the total mass of solids, destroys pathogens, and makes it easier to dewater or dry the sludge. Digested sludge is inoffensive, having the appearance and characteristics of a rich potting soil.

Most large sewage treatment plants use a two-stage digestion system in which organics are metabolized by bacteria anaerobically (in the absence of oxygen). In the first stage the sludge is heated and mixed in a closed tank for about 15 days, while digestion takes place. The sludge then flows into a second tank, which serves primarily for storage and settling. As the organic solids are broken down by anaerobic bacteria, carbon dioxide and methane gas are formed. Methane is combustible and is used as a fuel to heat the first digestion tank as well as to generate electricity for the plant. Anaerobic digestion is very sensitive to temperature, acidity, and other factors. It requires careful monitoring and control.

Sludge digestion may also take place aerobically—that is, in the presence of oxygen. The sludge is vigorously aerated in an open tank for about 20 days. Methane gas is not formed in this process. Although aerobic systems are easier to operate than anaerobic systems, they usually cost more to operate because of the power needed for aeration. Aerobic digestion is often combined with small extended aeration or contact stabilization systems.

Both aerobic and anaerobic digestion convert about half of the organic sludge solids to liquids and gases.

Dewatering

Digested sewage sludge is usually dewatered before disposal. Dewatered sludge still contains a significant amount of water—often as much as 70 percent—but, even with that moisture content, sludge no longer behaves as a liquid and can be handled as a solid material. Sludge-drying beds provide the simplest method of dewatering. A digested sludge slurry is spread on an open bed of sand and allowed to remain until dry. Drying takes place by a combination of evaporation and gravity drainage through the sand. A piping network built under the sand collects the water, which is pumped back to the head of the plant. After about six weeks of drying, the sludge cake, as it is called, may have a solids content of about 40 percent. It can then be removed from the sand with a pitchfork or a front-end loader. In order to reduce drying time in wet or cold weather, a glass enclosure may be built over the sand beds. Since a good deal of land area is needed for drying beds, this method of dewatering is commonly used in rural or suburban towns rather than in densely populated cities.

Alternatives to sludge-drying beds include the rotary drum vacuum filter, the centrifuge, and the belt filter press. These mechanical systems require less space than do sludge-drying beds, and they offer a greater degree of operational control. However, they usually have to be preceded by a step called sludge conditioning, in which chemicals are added to the liquid sludge to coagulate solids and improve drainability.

DISPOSAL

The final destination of treated sewage sludge usually is the land. Dewatered sludge can be buried underground in a sanitary landfill. It also may be spread on agricultural land in order to make use of its value as a soil conditioner and fertilizer. Since sludge may contain toxic industrial chemicals, it is not spread on land where crops are grown for human consumption.

Where a suitable site for land disposal is not available, as in urban areas, sludge may be incinerated. Incineration completely evaporates the moisture and converts the organic solids into inert ash. The ash must be disposed of, but the reduced volume makes disposal more economical. Air pollution control is a very important consideration when sewage sludge is incinerated. Appropriate air-cleaning devices such as scrubbers and filters must be used.

Dumping sludge in the ocean, once an economical disposal method for many coastal communities, is no longer considered a viable option. It is now prohibited in the United States.

CHAPTER 8
OTHER FORMS OF POLLUTION

In addition to being defined by the environment (air, water, and land) that is being despoiled, pollution can be identified by the material or energy that is being projected into the environment. Such is the case with noise pollution, light pollution, plastic pollution, and radioactive waste—forms of pollution that are being encountered with greater frequency in modern life and that periodically have aroused great public concern.

NOISE POLLUTION

Noise pollution is unwanted or excessive sound that can have deleterious effects on human health and environmental quality. Commonly generated inside many industrial facilities and some other workplaces, noise pollution also comes from highway, railway, and airplane traffic and from outdoor construction activities.

MEASURING AND PERCEIVING LOUDNESS

Sound waves are vibrations of air molecules carried from a noise source to the ear. Sound is typically described in terms of the loudness (amplitude) and the pitch (frequency) of the wave. Loudness (also called sound pressure level, or SPL) is measured in logarithmic units called decibels (dB). The normal human ear can detect sounds that range between 0 dB (hearing threshold) and about 140 dB (pain threshold). The ambient SPL in a library is about 35 dB, while that inside a moving bus or subway train is roughly 85 dB; building construction activities can generate SPLs as high as 105 dB at the source. SPLs decrease with distance from the source.

The rate at which sound energy is transmitted, called sound intensity, is proportional to the square of the SPL. Because of the logarithmic nature of the decibel scale, an increase of 10 dB represents a 10-fold increase in sound intensity, an increase of 20 dB represents a 100-fold increase in intensity, a 30-dB increase represents a 1,000-fold increase in intensity, and so on. When sound intensity is doubled, on the other hand, the SPL increases by only 3 dB. For example, if a construction drill causes a noise level of about 90 dB, then two identical drills operating side by side will cause a noise level of 93 dB. On the other hand, when two sounds that differ by more than 15 dB in SPL are combined, the weaker sound is masked (or drowned out) by the louder sound. For example, if an 80-dB drill is operating next to a 95-dB dozer at a construction site, the combined SPL of those two sources will be measured as 95 dB; the less intense sound from the compressor will not be noticeable.

Frequency of a sound wave is expressed in cycles per second (cps), but hertz (Hz) is more commonly used (1 cps = 1 Hz). The human eardrum is a very sensitive organ with a large dynamic range, being able to detect sounds at frequencies as low as 20 Hz (a very low pitch) up to about 20,000 Hz (a very high pitch). The pitch of a human voice in normal conversation occurs at frequencies between 250 Hz and 2,000 Hz.

Precise measurement and scientific description of sound levels differ from most subjective human perceptions and opinions about sound. Subjective human responses to noise depend on both pitch and loudness. People with normal hearing generally perceive high-frequency sounds to be louder than low-frequency sounds of the same amplitude. For this reason electronic sound-level meters used to measure noise levels take into account the variations of perceived loudness with pitch. Frequency filters in the meters serve to match meter readings with the sensitivity of the human ear and the relative loudness of various sounds. The so-called A-weighted filter, for example, is commonly used for measuring ambient community noise. SPL measurements made with this filter are expressed as A-weighted decibels, or dBA. Most people perceive and describe a 6- to 10-dBA increase in an SPL reading to be a doubling of "loudness."

Noise levels generally vary with time, so noise measurement data are reported as time-averaged values to express overall noise levels. There are several ways to do this. For example, the results of a set of repeated sound-level measurements may be reported as L_{90} = 75 dBA, meaning that the levels were equal to or higher than 75 dBA for 90 percent of the time. Another unit, called equivalent sound levels (L_{eq}), can be used to express an average SPL over any period of interest, such as an eight-hour workday. (L_{eq} is a logarithmic average rather than an arithmetic average, so loud events prevail in the overall result.) A unit called day-night sound level (DNL or L_{dn}) accounts for the fact that people are more sensitive to noise during the night, so a 10-dBA penalty is added to SPL values that are measured between 10 pm and 7 am. DNL measurements are very useful for describing overall community exposure to aircraft noise, for example.

Dealing with the Effects of Noise

Noise can be more than a mere nuisance. At certain levels and durations of exposure, it can cause physical damage to the eardrum and result in temporary or permanent hearing loss. Hearing loss does not usually occur at SPLs below 80 dBA (eight-hour exposure levels are best kept below 85 dBA) but most people repeatedly exposed to more than 105 dBA will have permanent hearing loss to some extent.

In addition to causing hearing loss, excessive noise exposure can also raise blood pressure and pulse rates, cause irritability, anxiety, and mental fatigue, and interfere with sleep, recreation, and personal communication. Noise pollution control is therefore of importance in the workplace and in the community. Noise-control ordinances and laws enacted at the local, regional, and national levels can be effective in mitigating the adverse effects of noise pollution.

Environmental noise and industrial noise are regulated in the United States under the Occupational Safety and Health Act of 1970 and the Noise Control Act of 1972. Under these acts, the Occupational Safety and Health Administration has set up industrial noise criteria in order to provide limits on the intensity of sound exposure and on the time duration for which that intensity may be allowed. Maximum daily exposure to noise at various levels is given in the table on the following page. If an individual is exposed to various levels of noise for different time intervals during the day, the total exposure or dose (D) of noise is obtained from the relation

$$D = (C_1/T_1) + (C_2/T_2) + (C_3/T_3) + ...,$$

where C is the actual time of exposure and T is the allowable time of exposure at any level in the table. Using this formula, the maximum allowable daily noise dose will be 1, and any daily exposure over 1 is unacceptable.

Criteria for indoor noise are summarized in three sets of specifications that have been derived by collecting subjective judgments from a large sampling of people in a variety of specific situations. These have developed into the noise criteria (NC) and preferred noise criteria (PNC) curves, which provide limits on the level of noise introduced into the environment. The NC curves, developed in

DAILY MAXIMUM NOISE EXPOSURE PERMITTED BY THE U.S. OCCUPATIONAL SAFETY AND HEALTH ACT OF 1970	
SOUND LEVEL (DECIBELS)	**MAXIMUM HOURS PER DAY**
115	<¼
110	½
105	1
100	2
97	3
95	4
92	6
90	8

1957, aim to provide a comfortable working or living environment by specifying the maximum allowable level of noise in octave bands over the entire audio spectrum. The complete set of 11 curves specifies noise criteria for a broad range of situations. The PNC curves, developed in 1971, add limits on low-frequency rumble and high-frequency hiss; hence, they are preferred over the older NC standard. Summarized in the curves shown in the figure, these criteria provide design goals for noise levels for a variety of different purposes. Part of the specification of a work or living environment is the appropriate PNC curve; in the event that the sound level exceeds PNC limits, sound-absorptive materials can be introduced into the environment as necessary to meet the appropriate standards.

Low levels of noise may be overcome using additional absorbing material, such as heavy drapery or sound-absorbent tiles in enclosed rooms. Where low levels of identifiable noise may be distracting, or where privacy of conversations in adjacent offices and reception areas may be important, the undesirable sounds may be masked. A small white-noise source such as static or rushing air, placed in the room, can mask the sounds of conversation from adjacent rooms without being offensive or dangerous to the ears of people working nearby. This type of device is often used in offices of doctors and other professionals. Another technique for reducing personal noise level is through the use of hearing protectors, which are held over the ears in the same manner as an earmuff. By using commercially available earmuff-type hearing protectors, a decrease in sound level can be attained ranging typically from about 10 decibels at 100 hertz to over 30 decibels for frequencies above 1,000 hertz.

Outdoor noise limits are also important for human comfort. Standard house construction will provide some shielding from external sounds if the house meets minimum standards of construction and if the outside noise level falls within acceptable limits. These limits are generally specified for particular periods of the day—for example, during daylight hours, during evening hours, and at night during sleeping hours. Because of refraction in the atmosphere owing to the nighttime temperature inversion, relatively loud sounds can be introduced into an area from a rather distant highway, airport, or railroad.

One interesting technique for control of highway noise is the erection of noise barriers alongside the highway, separating the highway from adjacent residential areas. The effectiveness of such barriers is limited by the diffraction of sound, which is greater at the lower frequencies that often predominate in road noise, especially from large vehicles. In order to be effective, they must be as close as possible to either the source or the observer of the noise (preferably to the source), thus maximizing the diffraction that would be necessary for the sound to reach

THE CAR MUFFLER

An automobile muffler is a device through which the exhaust gases are passed in order to attenuate, or reduce, the airborne noise of the engine. To be efficient as a sound reducer, a muffler must decrease the velocity of the exhaust gases and either absorb sound waves or cancel them by interference with reflected waves coming from the same source.

A typical sound-absorbing material used in a muffler is a thick layer of fine fibres; the fibres are caused to vibrate by the sound waves, thus converting the sound energy to heat. Mufflers of the straight-through type have a single tube with small holes connecting with annular chambers that are frequently stuffed with a sound-absorbing material.

Mufflers that attenuate sound waves by interference are known as reactive mufflers. These devices generally separate the waves into two

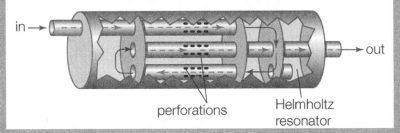

Noise flow through a typical muffler. In the typical reactive design shown in the illustration, the arrows indicate the flow of exhaust gas through a set of tubes and chambers inside the muffler. Encyclopædia Britannica, Inc.

components that follow different paths and then come together again out of phase (out of step), thus canceling each other out and reducing the sound. One important chamber is known as the Helmholtz resonator. This chamber is of a dimension carefully tuned to reflect and cancel sound waves of specified frequencies. In addition, the tubes can be perforated with small holes that allow the reflection and interference of sound waves of other frequencies. The result is the attenuation of sound across a range of desired frequencies.

the observer. Another requirement for this type of barrier is that it must also limit the amount of transmitted sound in order to bring about significant noise reduction.

LIGHT POLLUTION

Like noise pollution, light pollution—unwanted or excessive artificial light—is a form of waste energy that can cause adverse effects and degrade environmental quality. Moreover, because light (transmitted as electromagnetic waves) is typically generated by electricity, which itself is usually generated by the combustion of fossil fuels, it can be said that there is a connection between light pollution and air pollution (from fossil-fueled power plant emissions). Control of light pollution therefore will help to conserve fuel (and money) and reduce air pollution as well as mitigate the more immediate problems caused by the excessive light. Although light pollution may not appear to be as harmful to public health and welfare as pollution of water resources or the atmosphere, it is an environmental quality issue of no small significance.

Light pollution adversely affects professional and amateur astronomers, as well as casual observers of the night sky, because it severely reduces the visibility of stars and other celestial objects. The reduction in night sky visibility is a result of "skyglow," upward-directed light emanating from poorly designed or directed lamps and security floodlights. This wasted light is scattered and reflected by solid or liquid particles in the atmosphere and then returned to the eyes of people on the ground, obliterating their view of the night sky. The effect of skyglow from a town or city is not necessarily localized; it can be observed far from the main source.

Light pollution is a problem not only for astronomers and people who simply want to enjoy the beauty of a starry night. Glare from road lamps, commercial security lights and signs, or even from a neighbour's bright and misdirected yard lighting can cause discomfort and distraction and adversely affect the quality of life of many people. Light pollution also has adverse impacts on birds and other animals. Many migratory birds, for example, fly by night, when light from the stars and Moon helps them navigate. These birds are disoriented by the glare of artificial light as they fly over urban and suburban areas. It has been estimated by the American Bird Conservatory that more than four million migratory birds perish each year in the United States by colliding with brightly illuminated towers and buildings. Light pollution is considered to be one of the contributing factors in the dramatic decline of certain migratory songbird populations over the past several decades.

The quantity of light pollution from a given area depends on the number and brightness of light sources on the ground, the fraction of light that escapes above the horizontal, the reflectivity of surfaces near the light sources (e.g., roads, pavements, walls, windows), and the prevailing atmospheric conditions. Empirical formulas allow the calculation of skyglow levels as a function of population and distance from the observer. When skyglow levels are more than 10 percent above the natural background levels, significant sky degradation has begun. Even lights from a fairly small town with a population of only 3,000 people will cause significant night sky degradation for an observer as far as 10 km (6 miles) away.

Light pollution can be reduced by using well-designed light fixtures with modern optical controls to direct the light downward and also by using the minimum amount of wattage for the area to be illuminated. National and local government agencies can help by passing and enforcing appropriate light-control laws and ordinances.

PLASTIC POLLUTION

In 1907 the invention of Bakelite brought about a revolution in materials by introducing truly synthetic plastic resins into world commerce. By the end of the 20th century, however, plastics were found to be persistent polluters of many environmental niches, from Mount Everest to the bottom of the sea. Whether being mistaken for food by animals, flooding low-lying areas by clogging drainage systems, or simply causing significant aesthetic blight, plastics have attracted increasing attention as a large-scale pollutant.

The Problem of Plastics

Plastic is a polymeric material—that is, a material whose molecules are very large, often resembling long chains made up of a seemingly endless series of interconnected links. Natural polymers such as rubber and silk exist in abundance, but nature's "plastics" have not been implicated in environmental pollution, because they do not persist in the environment. Today, however, the average consumer comes into daily contact with all kinds of manmade plastic materials that have been developed specifically to defeat natural decay processes—materials derived mainly from petroleum that can be molded, cast, spun, or applied as a coating.

Since synthetic plastics are largely nonbiodegradable, they tend to persist in natural environments. Moreover, many lightweight, single-use plastic products and packaging materials, which account for approximately 50 percent of all plastics produced, are not deposited in containers for subsequent removal to landfills, recycling centres, or incinerators. Instead, they are improperly disposed of at or near the location where they end their usefulness to the consumer. Dropped on the ground, thrown out of a car window, heaped onto an already full rubbish bin, or inadvertently carried off by a gust of wind, they immediately begin to pollute the environment.(Illegal dumping of plastic and overflowing of containment structures also play a role.) Indeed, landscapes littered by plastic packaging have become common in many parts of the world. Studies have not shown any particular country or demographic group to be most responsible, though population centres generate the most litter.

According to the trade association PlasticsEurope, world plastic production grew from some 1.5 million tons in 1950 to an estimated 260 million tons in 2007. Compared with materials in common use in the first half of the 20th century, such as glass, paper, iron, and aluminum, plastics have a low recovery rate. In other words, they are relatively inefficient to reuse as recycled scrap in the manufacturing process, due to significant processing difficulties such as a low melting point, which prevents contaminants from being driven off during heating and reprocessing. Most recycled plastics are subsidized below the cost of raw materials by various deposit schemes, or their recycling is simply mandated by government regulations. Recycling rates vary dramatically from country to country, with only northern European countries obtaining rates greater than 50 percent. In any case, recycling does not really address plastic pollution, since recycled plastic is "properly" disposed of, whereas plastic pollution comes from improper disposal.

Plastic Pollution in Oceans and on Land

Since the ocean is downstream from nearly every terrestrial location, it is the receiving body for much of the plastic waste generated on land. It has been estimated

Piles of plastic waste removed from a Hong Kong beach. The debris most likely washed ashore from the South Pacific Subtropical Gyre, which contains a floating "garbage patch" of discarded plastic. Antony Dickson/AFP/ Getty Images

that 6.4 million tons of debris end up in the world's oceans every year and that some 60 to 80 percent of that debris, or 3.8 to 5 million tons, is improperly discarded plastic litter. Plastic pollution was first noticed in the ocean by scientists carrying out plankton studies in the late 1960s and early 1970s, and oceans and beaches still receive most of the attention of those studying and working to abate plastic pollution. Floating plastic waste has been shown to accumulate in five subtropical gyres that cover 40 percent of the world's oceans. Located at Earth's midlatitudes, these gyres include the North and South Pacific Subtropical Gyres, whose eastern "garbage patches" (zones with high concentrations of plastic waste circulating near the ocean surface) have garnered the attention of scientists and the media. The other gyres are the North and South Atlantic Subtropical Gyres and the Indian Ocean Subtropical Gyre.

In the ocean, plastic pollution can kill marine mammals directly through entanglement in objects such as fishing gear, but it can also kill through ingestion, by being mistaken for food. Studies have found that all kinds of species, including small zooplankton, large cetaceans, most seabirds, and all marine turtles, readily ingest plastic bits and trash items such as cigarette lighters, plastic bags, and bottle caps. Sunlight and seawater embrittle plastic, and the eventual breakdown of larger objects makes it available to zooplankton and other small marine animals. In addition to being nonnutritive and indigestible, plastics have been shown to concentrate pollutants up to a million times their level in the surrounding seawater and then deliver them to the species that ingest them. In one study, levels of polychlorinated biphenyl (PCB), a lubricant and insulating material that is now widely banned, were shown to have increased significantly in the preen gland oil of streaked shearwaters (*Calonectris leucomelas*) after these seabirds had been fed plastic pellets culled from Tokyo Bay for only one week.

There are also terrestrial aspects to plastic pollution. Drainage systems become clogged with plastic bags, films, and other items, causing flooding. Land birds, such as the reintroduced California condor, have been found with plastic in their stomachs, and animals that normally feed in waste dumps—for instance, the sacred cows of India— have had intestinal blockages from plastic packaging. The mass of plastic is not greater than that of other major components of waste, but it takes up a disproportionately large volume. As waste dumps expand in residential areas, the scavenging poor are often found living near or even on piles of residual plastics.

POLLUTION BY PLASTICS ADDITIVES

Plastic also pollutes without being littered—specifically, through the release of compounds used in its manufacture. Indeed, pollution of the environment by chemicals leached from plastics into air and water is an emerging area of concern. As a result, some compounds used in plastics, such as phthalates, bisphenol A (BPA), and polybrominated diphenyl ether (PBDE), have come under close scrutiny and regulation. Phthalates are plasticizers—softeners used to make plastic products less brittle. They are found in medical devices, food packaging, automobile upholstery, flooring materials, and computers as well as in pharmaceuticals, perfumes, and cosmetics. BPA, used in the manufacture of clear, hard polycarbonate plastics and strong epoxy coatings and adhesives, is present in packaging, bottles, compact discs, medical devices, and the linings of food cans. PBDE is added to plastics as a flame retardant. All these compounds have been detected in humans and are known to disrupt the endocrine system. Phthalates act against male hormones and are therefore known as anti-androgens. BPA mimics the natural female hormone estrogen, and PBDE has been shown to disrupt thyroid hormones in addition to being an anti-androgen. The people most vulnerable to such hormone-disrupting chemicals are children and women of reproductive age.

These compounds have also been implicated in hormone disruption of animals in terrestrial, aquatic, and marine habitats. Effects are seen in laboratory animals at blood levels lower than those found in the average resident of a developed country. Amphibians, mollusks, worms, insects, crustaceans, and fish show effects on their reproduction and development, including alterations in the number of offspring produced, disruption of larval development, and (in insects) delayed emergence, although studies investigating resulting declines in those populations have not been reported. Studies are needed to fill this knowledge gap, as are studies of the effects of exposure to mixtures of those compounds on animals and humans.

SOLVING THE PROBLEM

Given the global scale of plastic pollution, the cost of removing plastics from the environment would be prohibitive. Most solutions to the problem of plastic pollution, therefore, focus on preventing improper disposal or even on limiting the use of certain plastic items in the first place. Fines for littering have proved difficult to enforce, but various fees or outright bans on foamed food containers and plastic shopping bags are now common, as are deposits redeemed by taking beverage bottles to recycling centres. So-called extended producer responsibility, or EPR, schemes make the manufacturers of some items responsible for creating an infrastructure to take back and recycle the products that they produce. Awareness of the serious consequences of plastic pollution is increasing, and new solutions, including the increasing use of biodegradable plastics and a "zero waste" philosophy, are being embraced by governments and the public.

RADIOACTIVE WASTE

Some 20 percent of the electricity generated in the United States originates in nuclear power plants. At the core of a nuclear power plant is the nuclear reactor, a device that can initiate and control a self-sustaining series of nuclear fissions. Fission is the process in which a heavy nucleus splits into two smaller fragments. A large amount of energy is released in this process, and this energy is the basis of the power plant. The heat released by fission is removed

The view from homes near the Exelon Bryon nuclear power plant in Byron, Ill. The disposal of nuclear waste and the potential for radiation exposure are considered pollution threats. Jeff Haynes/AFP/Getty Images

from the reactor core by a coolant circulated through the core. Some of the thermal energy in the coolant is used to heat water and convert it to high-pressure steam. This steam drives a turbine, and the turbine's mechanical energy is then converted into electricity by means of a generator.

Most of the energy of fission—about 85 percent of it—is released within a very short time after the process occurs. The rest of the energy comes from the radioactive decay of fission products. Radioactive decay continues when the fission reaction has been stopped, and its energy must be dealt with in any proper reactor design. In particular, significant measures must be taken to prevent the exposure of living tissue to the products of radioactive decay—namely, gamma rays, X-rays, and such high-energy particles as neutrons, electrons, and positrons—at all stages in the nuclear fuel cycle, from fabrication of fuel rods through controlled fission in the reactor core to the storage and disposal of spent fuel and other forms of radioactive waste.

Reactor Fuel

Reactor fuel consists of uranium dioxide that is ground into a very fine flour and sintered in a furnace to produce dense ceramic pellets. The pellets are then loaded into prefabricated zirconium alloy cladding tubes, which are filled with an inert gas and welded shut. These tubes, or pins, are bundled together with proper spacing assured by top and bottom grid plates through which the ends of the pins pass. Together with other necessary hardware, the bundle constitutes a fuel assembly. Fuel assemblies are loaded into a reactor in a careful pattern so as to obtain the most energy production from it before it becomes no longer usable. Typically, a reactor is fueled in cycles, each cycle lasting one to two years, and a fuel batch is kept in the reactor for three or four cycles. At the end of each cycle, spent fuel is removed and fresh fuel is loaded.

COOLING AND STORAGE OF FUEL AND WASTE

Spent reactor fuel is extremely radioactive, and its radioactivity also makes it a source of heat. A 1,000-megawatt nuclear power reactor produces on the order of 20–25 tons of spent fuel per year. Spent fuel is initially stored for up to several decades underwater in storage pools. This allows the high-activity, short-half-life radioactivity to decay. The water in the pool contains a large amount of dissolved boric acid, which is a heavy absorber of neutrons; this assures that the fuel assemblies in the pool will not go critical. (Pool water is also a common source of emergency cooling water for the reactor.) Pools vary in size; the older ones are able to accommodate only about 10 years worth of spent fuel. As the pools fill up, the oldest fuel assemblies are removed and stored in air-cooled concrete and steel silos located above ground. This so-called dry storage becomes feasible after fuel has been stored for two or three years because radioactivity and heat generation decrease rapidly over this period.

Some spent nuclear fuel can be reprocessed to recover reusable uranium and plutonium. However, the waste stream from this process also contains radioactive isotopes with much longer half-lives. It is widely accepted that this high-level waste (HLW) must be incorporated into a solid form prior to burial in deep geologic repositories. In most nuclear countries the accepted first-generation solid form for disposing of HLW is borosilicate glass. The waste solution is completely evaporated, leaving behind the fission products in the solid residue, which is heated until all the constituent nitrate salts are converted to oxides. These oxides are then put into a glass-forming oven and mixed with materials that will produce a boro-silicate glass. The fission-product oxides dissolve in the glass as it forms. The glass melt is subsequently poured into a steel canister, 200–400 mm in diameter and about one metre high, where it solidifies into a solid glass block. Once covered with an overpack of bentonite clay, the solid canister-like block is ready for disposal.

A more advanced second-generation form for storing HLW is synroc, a ceramic synthetic rock. Synroc contains various titanate-mineral phases that have the capability of forming solid solutions with nearly all the radioactive species in HLW. Similar minerals exist in nature, where they have survived under demanding conditions for geologic time periods.

The requirements of a nuclear waste form for HLW are rigorous. The waste form must be able to take into solid solution or at least to encapsulate the radioactive species. This is necessary so that the rate of leaching into underground water in a geologic repository will be acceptably low. Leach resistance must be maintained against deterioration of the waste form by radiation damage over long time periods, possibly lasting thousands of years. The form must be amenable to fabrication into large cylindrical monoliths, with minimal internal cracking. Other important considerations are low cost and personnel safety from such hazards as respirable dust and radiation exposure.

In addition to HLW, certain low-level wastes (LLW) accumulate in nuclear power facilities, hospitals, and research institutions. LLW includes such items as contaminated clothing, wiping rags, tools, test tubes, needles, and other medical research materials. These materials are reduced in volume, then packaged in leak-proof containers, which are either stored at the site where they originate or sent to a land disposal site.

LONG-TERM WASTE DISPOSAL

The waste disposal method currently being planned by all countries with nuclear power plants is called geologic disposal. This means that all conditioned nuclear wastes are to be deposited in mined cavities deep underground. Shafts are to be sunk into a solid rock stratum, with tunnel corridors extending horizontally from the central shaft region and tunnel "rooms" laterally from the corridors. The waste would be emplaced (probably by remotely controlled or robotic devices) in holes drilled into the floors of these rooms, after which the boreholes would be sealed and the rooms and corridors backfilled. When the entire operation is completed (perhaps after about 30 years of operation), the shafts too would be backfilled and sealed.

Nuclear waste retains its very intense level of radioactivity for several hundred years, but after 1,000 years have passed the remaining radioactivity, while persistent, is at a level comparable to, but greater than, that of a body of natural uranium ore. This separates the safety problem into two time periods: a first millennium during which it is crucial to ensure tight retention of the wastes in the repository, and a subsequent period during which it is only necessary to ensure that any release that occurs is small and slow.

Finally, a great deal of care is to be expended in selecting the site of the repository. Site selection is probably the biggest problem, both politically and technically. Various conditions are mandatory. The repository must not be near a populated area, the rock stratum selected must be deep (300 metres [984 ft] or more) and, as much as possible, naturally sealed from aquifers. Also, any discharge of the water table into the surface waters should be slow. Furthermore, the site must be in a tectonically inactive zone so that earthquakes will not break that seal.

RADIATION SICKNESS

The biomedical effects of ionizing radiation were made clear in 1945, when atomic bombs were dropped on Japan. In the immediate aftermath of the bombings and over the following years, the lasting effects of those weapons are known to have been responsible for tens of thousands of deaths due to radiation injury. Today nearly all cases of radiation sickness result from medical or industrial accidents and overexposures.

Great destruction or changes to tissue can be caused by exposure to the gamma rays, X-rays, and high-energy subatomic particles that make up ionizing radiation. The main structures affected are cells. Radiation energy is not spread diffusely throughout the tissue; rather, the energy rays penetrate into localized areas of tissue, affecting only the cells contacted by the rays. Whether a cell dies immediately or develops molecular changes depends upon the dose of radiation and the length of exposure.

Molecular changes in a cell are reflected in its ability to grow and divide to form a normal generation of daughter cells. When the radiation dose is high, cell death is rapid and extensive; there is usually no reserve tissue left to replace that which is destroyed. If the cell changes are more subtle, the cell may be unable to reproduce altogether or the new cells produced may be abnormal and not viable.

The tissues most affected by radiation are those that undergo rapid replacement, such as bone marrow, the lining of the gastrointestinal tract, and skin. Slower-growing tissues, such as those of the brain and liver, require either high doses of radiation or prolonged exposure before they show symptoms of degeneration. The overall direct complications of radiation are cell depletion, inability to reproduce new tissue, lessened body resistance to infections, decreased numbers of blood cells, hemorrhages from disrupted blood vessels, body poisons from tissue breakdown, and a slower blood-clotting time. Indirect effects can be tumour growths, leukemia, a shortened life span, recurrent bacterial infections, anemia, and body ulcers.

Local tissue injuries from radiation may manifest a number of months after the initial exposure or several years after a sequence of exposures. The skin may ulcerate, scale, swell, and slowly deteriorate. Systemic symptoms appear only after the whole body or numerous parts of it have been exposed.

Radiation sickness with systemic symptoms can exhibit four stages in milder cases or cause immediate convulsions, high blood pressure, shock, fever, skin reddening, and death. The first phase in the slower form develops within a few minutes or hours after exposure; symptoms are nausea, vomiting, weakness, and diarrhea. A day or two after exposure, the symptoms depart, and there is a second phase of apparent recovery that may last a week or longer. Third-stage symptoms are fever, infection, vomiting, bloody diarrhea, hemorrhages, dehydration, weight loss, hair loss, and ulcers. Death usually occurs in this phase if the damage has been sufficiently severe. If the patient survives the third phase, the fourth phase (slow recovery) begins about six weeks after the exposure. The recovery may take several months, and there may be permanent disability, such as sterilization, extensive scar tissue, cataracts, bone disintegration, cancer, and blindness.

The risk of high-level waste burial is almost certainly smaller than the risks of reactor accidents and even than the risks arising from improperly managed mine tailings. Nonetheless, the siting of a repository must be handled with political sensitivity, and the confirmation of acceptable hydrologic and geologic conditions must have a high degree of validity. There are many acceptable sites in principle, but confirming acceptability for any one of them is a large and expensive technical undertaking. In the United States, for example, a proposed nuclear-waste repository to be located deep within Yucca Mountain in Nevada was a source of controversy from the time the site was designated by the federal government in 1987. Opposition to the repository was aroused by fears that storage plans and environmental regulations were inadequate to protect against radioactive contamination of the groundwater, and federal approval of the site took some 15 years to accomplish. In 2002 the U.S. Senate authorized the building of the facility, but political and legal opposition was so strong that the federal government did not complete its application for a license to build and run the repository until 2008. By that time the project was projected to cost some $100 billion, and the facility was not expected to begin receiving spent fuel and high-level waste until 2020. Finally in 2010 the government stopped the project for budgetary reasons.

REACTOR SAFETY

Nuclear reactors contain very large amounts of radioactive isotopes — mostly fission products but also such heavy elements as plutonium. If this radioactivity were to escape the reactor, its effects on the people in the vicinity would be severe. The deleterious effects of exposure to high levels of ionizing radiation would include increased rates of cancer and genetic defects, an increased number of developmental abnormalities in children exposed in the womb, and even death within a period of several days to months when irradiation is extreme. For this reason, a major consideration in reactor design is ensuring that a significant release of radioactivity does not occur. This is accomplished by a combination of preventive measures and mitigating measures.

Preventive measures are those that are taken to avoid accidents, and mitigating measures are those that decrease the adverse consequences. Essentially, preventive measures are the set of design and operating rules that are intended to make certain that the reactor is operated safely, while mitigating measures are systems and structures that prevent such accidents as do occur from proceeding to a catastrophic conclusion. Among the most well-known preventive measures are the reports and inspections for double-checking that a plant is properly constructed, rules of operation, and qualification tests for operating personnel to ensure that they know their jobs. The mitigating measures include safety rod systems for quickly shutting down a reactor to prevent a runaway chain reaction; emergency cooling systems for removing the heat of radioactive decay in the event that normal cooling capability is lost; and the containment structure for confining any radioactivity that might escape the primary reactor system. An extreme mitigating measure is the exercising of plans to evacuate personnel who might otherwise be heavily exposed in a reactor installation.

PREVENTIVE MEASURES

Since no human activity can be shown to be absolutely safe, all these measures cannot reduce the risks to zero, but it is the aim of the rules and safety systems to minimize the risk to the point where a reasonable individual would conclude they are trivial. What this *de minimis* risk value is, and whether it has been achieved by the nuclear industry, is a subject of bitter controversy, but it is generally accepted that independent regulatory agencies—the United States Nuclear Regulatory Commission (NRC) and similar agencies around the world—are the proper judges of such matters.

To help evaluate the risks from nuclear power plants, the U.S. Atomic Energy Commission (AEC) authorized a major safety study in 1972 (the AEC was disbanded in 1974 and its functions have been assumed by the NRC). The study was conducted with major assistance from a number of laboratories, and it involved the application of probabilistic risk assessment (PRA) techniques for the first time on a system as complex as a large nuclear power reactor. This work resulted in the publication in 1975 of a report titled *Reactor Safety Study*, also known as WASH-1400.

The most useful aspect of the study was its delineation of components and accident sequences (scenarios)

that were determined to be the most significant contributors to severe accidents. The *Reactor Safety Study*
concluded that the risks of an accident that would injure
a large number of people were extremely low for the
light-water reactor systems analyzed. This conclusion,
however, was subject to very large quantitative uncer-
tainties and was challenged.

One basic problem with probabilistic risk assessment
is that it cannot easily be confirmed by experience when
the level of risk has been reduced to low values. That is to
say, if probabilistic risk assessment predicts that a reactor
is subject to, say, one failure in 10,000 years, there is no
way to prove that statement with only a few, or even with
10,000, years of experience. Thus, the results of the
Reactor Safety Study as to risk levels were not confirmable.

One area where probabilistic risk assessment has
proved useful is with regard to the licensing of new plants,
either light-water reactor installations or those of less
common reactor types. PRA has the virtue of comparing
systems fairly reliably. With better computer hardware
and software than were available in 1975, it has become
feasible to do PRA analyses of individual plants and com-
pare them. A standard protocol for the NRC in licensing
new, and particularly new types of, plants has therefore
been that they must demonstrate lower risks than light-
water reactors, which have been accepted as the norm.

Because all such nuclear plant accidents have basically resulted from human failings rather than from some
intrinsic factor, most experts believe that nuclear energy
can be a safe source of power. A review of the overall per-
formance record shows that there have been several
thousand "reactor-years" of safe power-reactor operation in the world, with health effects less damaging than
those associated with the extraction of an equal amount
of power from coal. Incorporating the lessons learned

CHERNOBYL

The significance of the human element, particularly as it relates to plant management and high-level regulatory decision making, was borne out again by the Chernobyl catastrophe of 1986. One of the four reactors in a nuclear power station about 100 km (62 miles) north of Kiev, Ukraine (then part of the Soviet Union), exploded and caught fire as the result of an ill-conceived experiment (a test to see how long the steam turbines would run while coasting to a stop if the reactor would be abruptly shut down). Before the situation had been brought under control, an estimated 25 percent of the radioactive contents of the reactor had been released in a high cloud plume, 116,000 people had to be evacuated, and a large area surrounding the plant received fallout so great that it could not be farmed or pastured. Significant radiation was detected as far north as Scandinavia and as far west as Switzerland.

Investigation of the accident placed the largest blame, as with the Three Mile Island mishap, on poor management both at the plant and within the government bureaucracy. In September 2005 the Chernobyl Forum, comprising seven UN organizations and programs, the World Bank, and the governments of Belarus, Russia, and Ukraine, published a three-volume, 600-page report assessing the impact on public health of the accident. Approximately 50 emergency workers died of acute radiation sickness shortly after the accident, and 9 children died from thyroid cancer because of radiation exposure. As a result of the accident, an additional 3,940 people—from among the 200,000 emergency workers who were present at the site in the first year following the accident, the people who were evacuated, and the 270,000 residents of the most heavily contaminated areas—were likely to die from cancer.

from past accidents should certainly make future operations safer.

There is, however, a condition on the conclusion that nuclear power is by and large a safe form of power. The facilities for generating this power must be designed, built, and operated to high standards by knowledgeable, well-trained professionals. Additionally, a regulatory mechanism capable of enforcing these standards must be in place.

Mitigating Measures

Two of the principal safety measures, the safety rods and the containment structure, have already been described. Other major safety systems are the emergency core cooling system, which makes it possible to cool the reactor if normal cooling is disrupted, and the emergency power system, which is designed to supply electrical power in case the normal supply is disrupted so that detectors and vital pumps and valves can continue to be operated. An important part of the safety system is the strict adherence to design rules, some of which have been mentioned—namely, the reactor should have a negative power-reactivity coefficient; the safety rods must be injectable under all circumstances; and no single regulating rod should be able to add substantial reactivity rapidly. Another important design rule is that the structural materials used in the reactor must retain acceptable physical properties over their expected service life. Finally, construction is to be covered by stringent quality assurance rules, and both design and construction must be in accordance with standards set by major engineering societies and accepted by the NRC.

According to probabilistic risk assessment studies, three kinds of events are most responsible for the risks associated with light-water reactors—namely, station blackout, transient without scram, and loss of cooling. The

Three Mile Island

The ultimate event in the chain that led to the Three Mile Island accident was loss of emergency cooling by operator action owing to a misinterpretation of what sort of accident was occurring. In 1979, Unit 2 of the Three Mile Island nuclear facility suffered a severe accident. Through a combination of operator errors, coupled with the failure of an important valve to operate correctly, cooling water to the core was lost, parts of the core were melted, and the rest of it destroyed. A large quantity of fission products was released from the primary reactor system to the interior of the containment structure. The containment vessel of the reactor building fulfilled its function, and only a small amount of radioactivity was released, demonstrating the wisdom of having this component. Still, a severe accident had occurred.

Many investigations of the Three Mile Island accident followed. Recommendations differed among them, but a common thread was that the human element was a much more important factor in safe operation than had been theretofore recognized. The human element pertained not only to the operating staff but also to the management of nuclear plants and even to the NRC itself. Following the accident, therefore, many changes in operator training and in technical and inspectorate staffing were implemented, just as a number of hardware enhancements were introduced. It is generally believed that these changes have been effective in reducing the likelihood of the occurrence of accidents as severe as that at Three Mile Island. As a side issue to this, however, the operating costs of nuclear power plants have escalated sharply as more and more highly trained people have been added to the operating staffs.

nature of each of these mishaps is delineated, as are the proposed countermeasures and the anticipated risks.

In station blackout, a failure in the power line to which the station is connected is postulated. The proposed emergency defense is a secondary electrical system, typically a combination of diesel generators big enough to drive the pumps and a battery supply sufficient to run the instruments. The risk would be that of the emergency generators not accepting load when they are started up. In transient without scram, the event is insertion of reactivity, for example, by an unchecked withdrawal of shim rods. The protective response is the rapid and automatic insertion of the safety rods. The risk would be the safety rods not functioning properly.

In loss of cooling, the event is a failure of the normal cooling system to operate, either because of a break in a coolant line or because of an operator error. The emergency response is activation of the emergency core cooling system, and the risk would be that the system fails to operate. In such cases, proper operator action and proper functioning of the appropriate backup system are important aspects of emergency response.

CHAPTER 9
WORKING TOWARD A NONPOLLUTING WORLD

O ne great difference between the world of today and the world of a century ago is the sensitivity shown by modern society to the danger posed by pollution. This growing sensitivity, or consciousness, on the part of society has expressed itself in various movements and professions dedicated to preserving a healthy and sustainable environment.

One example is environmental law. Once a modest adjunct of the law of public health regulations, this branch of law developed during the late 20th century into an almost universally recognized independent field protecting both human health and nonhuman nature. Another example is environmental engineering, which was traditionally called sanitary engineering and was considered to be a specialized field within civil engineering. This began to change in the mid-1960s, when the more accurate name *environmental engineering* was adopted. The field today is concerned with designing all processes and maintaining all infrastructures that preserve the quality of the environment.

The massive social movement known today as environmentalism was dominated from the late 19th to the mid-20th century by middle-class lobbying groups in Europe and North America that were concerned mainly with nature conservation, wildlife protection, and pollution. Today the environmental movement has become a global force, largely through the establishment in the 1970s and '80s of "green" political parties, and has grown to have a major influence on the agenda of international politics.

ENVIRONMENTAL LAW

Environmental law has become a vast field that takes in all the principles, policies, directives, and regulations that are enacted and enforced by local, national, or international entities to regulate human treatment of the nonhuman world. Its influence is felt in diverse legal settings, such as state bottle-return laws in the United States, regulatory standards for emissions from coal-fired power plants in Germany, initiatives in China to create a "Green Great Wall"—a shelter belt of trees—to protect Beijing from sandstorms, and international treaties for the protection of biological diversity and the ozonosphere.

HISTORICAL DEVELOPMENT

Throughout history national governments have passed occasional laws to protect human health from environmental contamination. About 80 CE the Senate of Rome passed legislation to protect the city's supply of clean water for drinking and bathing. In the 14th century England prohibited both the burning of coal in London and the disposal of waste into waterways. In 1681 the Quaker leader of the English colony of Pennsylvania, William Penn, ordered that one acre of forest be preserved for every five acres cleared for settlement, and in the following century Benjamin Franklin led various campaigns to curtail the dumping of waste. In the 19th century, in the midst of the Industrial Revolution, the British government passed regulations to reduce the deleterious effects of coal burning and chemical manufacture on public health and the environment.

Prior to the 20th century there were few international environmental agreements. The accords that were reached focused primarily on boundary waters, navigation, and fishing rights along shared waterways and ignored pollution and other ecological issues. In the early 20th century, conventions to protect commercially valuable species were reached, including the Convention for the Protection of Birds Useful to Agriculture (1902), signed by 12 European governments; the Convention for the Preservation and Protection of Fur Seals (1911), concluded by the United States, Japan, Russia, and the United Kingdom; and the Convention for the Protection of Migratory Birds (1916), adopted by the United States and the United Kingdom (on behalf of Canada) and later extended to Mexico in 1936. In the 1930s Belgium, Egypt, Italy, Portugal, South Africa, Sudan, and the United Kingdom adopted the Convention Relative to the Preservation of Fauna and Flora in their Natural State, which committed those countries to preserve natural fauna and flora in Africa by means of national parks and reserves. Spain and France signed the convention but never ratified it, and Tanzania formally adopted it in 1962. India, which acceded to the agreement in 1939, was subject to the sections of the document prohibiting "trophies" made from any animal mentioned in the annex.

Beginning in the 1960s, environmentalism became an important political and intellectual movement in the West. In the United States the publication of biologist Rachel Carson's *Silent Spring* (1962), a passionate and persuasive examination of chlorinated hydrocarbon pesticides and the environmental damage caused by their use, led to a reconsideration of a much broader range of actual and potential environmental hazards. In subsequent decades the U.S. government passed an extraordinary number of environmental laws—including acts addressing solid-waste disposal, air and water pollution, and the protection of endangered species—and created an Environmental Protection Agency to monitor compliance with them. These new environmental laws dramatically increased the national government's role in an area previously left primarily to state and local regulation.

In Japan rapid reindustrialization after World War II was accompanied by the indiscriminate release of industrial chemicals into the human food chain in certain areas. In the city of Minamata, for example, large numbers of people suffered mercury poisoning after eating fish that had been contaminated with industrial wastes. By the early 1960s the Japanese government had begun to consider a comprehensive pollution-control policy, and in 1967 Japan enacted the world's first such overarching law, the Basic Law for Environmental Pollution Control. Not until the end of the 20th century was Minamata declared mercury-free.

Thirty-four countries in 1971 adopted the Convention on Wetlands of International Importance Especially as Waterfowl Habitat, generally known as the Ramsar Convention for the city in Iran in which it was signed. The agreement, which entered into force in 1975, now has nearly 100 parties. It required all countries to designate at least one protected wetland area, and it recognized the important role of wetlands in maintaining the ecological equilibrium.

Following the United Nations Conference on the Human Environment, held in Stockholm in 1972, the UN established the United Nations Environment Programme (UNEP) as the world's principal international environmental organization. Although UNEP oversees many modern-day agreements, it has little power to impose or enforce sanctions on noncomplying parties. Nevertheless, a series of important conventions arose directly from the conference, including the Convention on the Prevention of Marine Pollution by Dumping of Wastes or Other Matter (1972) and the Convention on International Trade in Endangered Species of Wild Fauna and Flora (1973).

Until the Stockholm conference, European countries generally had been slow to enact legal standards for environmental protection—though there had been some exceptions, such as the passage of the conservationist Countryside Act in the United Kingdom in 1968. In October 1972, only a few months after the UN conference, the leaders of the European Community (EC) declared that the goal of economic expansion had to be balanced with the need to protect the environment. In the following year the European Commission, the EC's executive branch, produced its first Environmental Action Programme, and since that time European countries have been at the forefront of environmental policy making. In Germany, for example, public attitudes toward environmental protection changed dramatically in the early 1980s, when it became known that many German forests were being destroyed by acid rain. The environmentalist German Green Party, founded in 1980, won representation in the Bundestag (national parliament) for the first time in 1983 and since then has campaigned for stricter environmental regulations. By the end of the 20th century, the party had joined a coalition government and was responsible for developing and implementing Germany's extensive environmental policies. As a group, Germany, The Netherlands, and Denmark—the so-called "green troika"—established themselves as leading innovators in environmental law.

During the 1980s, the "transboundary effects" of environmental pollution in individual countries spurred negotiations on several international environmental conventions. The effects of the 1986 accident at the nuclear power plant at Chernobyl in Ukraine (then part of the Soviet Union) were especially significant. European countries in the pollution's downwind path were forced to adopt measures to restrict their populations' consumption of water, milk, meat, and vegetables. In Austria traces of radiation were found in cow's milk as well as in human breast milk. As a direct result of the Chernobyl disaster, two international agreements—the Convention on Early Notification of a Nuclear Accident and the Convention on Assistance in the Case of Nuclear Accident or Radiological Emergency, both adopted in 1986—were rapidly drafted to ensure notification and assistance in the event of a nuclear accident. In the following decade a Convention on Nuclear Safety (1994) established incentives for countries to adopt basic standards for the safe operation of land-based nuclear power plants.

There are often conflicting data about the environmental impact of human activities, and scientific uncertainty often has complicated the drafting and implementation of environmental laws and regulations, particularly for international conferences attempting to develop universal standards. Consequently, such laws and regulations usually are designed to be flexible enough to accommodate changes in scientific understanding and technological capacity. The Vienna Convention for the Protection of the Ozone Layer (1985), for example, did not specify the measures that signatory states were required to adopt to protect human health and the environment from the effects of ozone depletion, nor did it mention any of the substances that were thought to damage the ozone layer. Similarly, the Framework Convention on Climate Change, or Global Warming Convention, adopted by 178 countries meeting in Rio de Janeiro at the 1992 United Nations Conference on Environment and Development (popularly known as the "Earth Summit"), did not set binding targets for reducing the emission of the "greenhouse" gases thought to cause global warming.

In 1995 the Intergovernmental Panel on Climate Change, which was established by the World Meteorological Organization and UNEP to study changes in the Earth's temperature, concluded that "the balance of evidence suggests a discernible human influence on global climate." Although cited by environmentalists as final proof of the reality of global warming, the report was faulted by some critics for relying on insufficient data, for overstating the environmental impact of global warming, and for using unrealistic models of climate change.

Two years later in Kyoto, Japan, a conference of signatories to the Framework Convention on Climate Change adopted the Kyoto Protocol, which featured binding emission targets for developed countries. The protocol authorized developed countries to engage in emissions trading in order to meet their emissions targets. Its market mechanisms included the sale of "emission reduction units," which are earned when a developed country reduces its emissions below its commitment level, to developed countries that have failed to achieve their emission targets. Developed countries could earn additional emission reduction units by financing energy-efficient projects (e.g., clean-development mechanisms) in developing countries. Since its adoption, the protocol has encountered stiff opposition from some countries, particularly the United States, which has failed to ratify it.

Levels of Environmental Law

Environmental law exists at many levels and is only partly constituted by international declarations, conventions, and treaties. The bulk of environmental law is statutory (i.e., encompassed in the enactments of legislative bodies) and regulatory (i.e., generated by agencies charged by governments with protection of the environment).

In addition, many countries have included some right to environmental quality in their national constitutions. Since 1994, for example, environmental protection has been enshrined in the German Grundgesetz ("Basic Law"),

Dignitaries, including Chinese Prime Minister Zhu Rongji (rear-left) *and U.S. Vice President Al Gore* (rear-right), *attend the signing of an environmental agreement in 1999.* George Bridges/AFP/Getty Images

which now states that the government must protect for "future generations the natural foundations of life." Similarly, the Chinese constitution declares that the state "ensures the rational use of natural resources and protects rare animals and plants"; the South African constitution recognizes a right to "an environment that is not harmful to health or well-being; and to have the environment protected, for the benefit of present and future generations"; the Bulgarian constitution provides for a "right to a healthy and favourable environment, consistent with stipulated standards and regulations"; and the Chilean constitution contains a "right to live in an environment free from contamination."

Much environmental law also is embodied in the decisions of international, national, and local courts. Some of it is manifested in arbitrated decisions, such as the Trail

Smelter arbitration (1941), which enjoined the operation of a smelter located in British Columbia, Canada, near the international border with the U.S. state of Washington and held that "no State has the right to use or permit the use of its territory in such a manner as to cause injury by fumes in or to the territory of another or the properties or persons therein."

Some environmental law also appears in the decisions of national courts. For example, in *Scenic Hudson Preservation Conference* v. *Federal Power Commission* (1965), a U.S. federal appeals court voided a license granted by the Federal Power Commission for the construction of an environmentally damaging pumped-storage hydroelectric plant (i.e., a plant that would pump water from a lower to an upper reservoir) in an area of stunning natural beauty, demonstrating that the decisions of federal agencies could be successfully challenged in the courts. Significant local decisions included *National Audubon Society* v. *Superior Court* (1976), in which the California Supreme Court dramatically limited the ability of the Los Angeles to divert water that might otherwise fill Mono Lake in California's eastern desert.

Types of Environmental Law

Most environmental law falls into a general category of laws known as "command and control," which identify and regulate activities that are harmful to the environment. Another significant form of environmental law is environmental assessment mandates, which require that information be made publicly available on possible consequences to the environment of certain activities. Yet other types are the creation of economic incentives such as taxes and subsidies and the "setting aside" of areas deemed to be of ecological value.

Command-and-Control Legislation

Most environmental law falls into a general category of laws known as "command and control." Such laws typically involve three elements: (1) identification of a type of environmentally harmful activity, (2) imposition of specific conditions or standards on that activity, and (3) prohibition of forms of the activity that fail to comply with the imposed conditions or standards. The United States Federal Water Pollution Control Act (1972), for example, regulates "discharges" of "pollutants" into "navigable waters of the United States." All three terms are defined in the statute and agency regulations and together identify the type of environmentally harmful activity subject to regulation. In 1983 Germany passed a national emission-control law that set specific air emission thresholds by power plant age and type. Almost all environmental laws prohibit regulated activities that do not comply with stated conditions or standards. Many make a "knowing" (intentional) violation of such standards a crime.

The most obvious forms of regulated activity involve actual discharges of pollutants into the environment (e.g., air, water, and groundwater pollution). However, environmental laws also regulate activities that entail a significant risk of discharging harmful pollutants (e.g., the transportation of hazardous waste, the sale of pesticides, and logging). For actual discharges, environmental laws generally prescribe specific thresholds of allowable pollution. For activities that create a risk of discharge, environmental laws generally establish management practices to reduce that risk.

The standards imposed on actual discharges generally come in two forms: (1) environmental-quality, or ambient, standards, which fix the maximum amount of the regulated pollutant or pollutants tolerated in the receiving body of air or water; and (2) emission, or discharge, standards, which regulate the amount of the pollutant or pollutants that any "source" may discharge into the environment. Most comprehensive environmental laws impose both environmental-quality and discharge standards and endeavour to coordinate their use to achieve a stated environmental-quality goal. Environmental-quality goals can be either numerical or narrative. Numerical targets set a specific allowable quantity of a pollutant (e.g., 10 micrograms of carbon monoxide per cubic metre of air measured over an eight-hour period). Narrative standards require that the receiving body of air or water be suitable for a specific use (e.g., swimming).

The management practices prescribed for activities that create a risk of discharge are diverse and context-specific. The United States Resource Conservation and Recovery Act (1991), for example, requires drip pads for containers in which hazardous waste is accumulated or stored, and the United States Oil Pollution Act (1990) mandates that all oil tankers of a certain size and age operating in U.S. waters be double-hulled.

Another type of activity regulated by command-and-control legislation is environmentally harmful trade. Among the most-developed regulations are those on trade in wildlife. The Convention on International Trade in Endangered Species of Wild Fauna and Flora (CITES, 1973), for example, authorizes signatories to the convention to designate species "threatened with extinction which are or may be affected by trade." Once a plant or animal species has been designated as endangered, countries generally are bound to prohibit import or export of that species except in specific limited circumstances. In 1989 listing of the African elephant as a protected species effectively prohibited most trade in African ivory, which was subsequently banned by Kenya and the EC. By this time the United States already had banned trade in African ivory, listing the African elephant as a threatened species under its Federal Endangered Species Act (1978). Despite these measures, some countries either failed to prohibit ivory imports (e.g., Japan) or refused to prohibit ivory exports (e.g., Botswana, Namibia, South Africa, and Zimbabwe), and elephants continued to face danger from poachers and smugglers.

Environmental Assessment Mandates

Environmental assessment mandates are another significant form of environmental law. Such mandates generally perform three functions: (1) identification of a level or threshold of potential environmental impact at which a contemplated action is significant enough to require the preparation of an assessment; (2) establishment of specific goals for the assessment mandated; and (3) setting of requirements to ensure that the assessment will be considered in determining whether to proceed with the action as originally contemplated or to pursue an alternative action. Unlike command-and-control regulations, which may directly limit discharges into the environment, mandated environmental assessments protect the environment indirectly by increasing the quantity and quality of publicly available information on the environmental consequences of contemplated actions. This information potentially improves the decision making of government officials and increases the public's involvement in the creation of environmental policy.

The United States National Environmental Policy Act (1969) requires the preparation of an environmental impact statement for any "major federal action significantly affecting the quality of the human environment." The statement must analyze the environmental impact of the proposed action and consider a range of alternatives, including a so-called "no-action alternative." The statute and regulations imposed by the Council on Environmental Quality, which was established under the 1969 act to coordinate federal environmental initiatives, require federal agencies to wait until environmental impact statements have been completed before taking actions that would preclude alternatives.

Similarly, the European Union (EU) requires an environmental impact assessment for two types of projects. So-called "annex-I Projects" (e.g., oil refineries, toxic waste landfills, and thermal power stations with heat output of 300 or more megawatts) are generally subject to the requirement, and "annex-II Projects" (e.g., activities in chemical, food, textile, leather, wood, and paper industries) are subject to an environmental impact assessment only where "member states consider that their characteristics so require." Such assessments must describe and evaluate the direct and indirect effects of the project on humans, fauna, flora, soil, water, air, climate, and landscape and the interaction between them.

Economic Incentives

The use of economic instruments to create incentives for environmental protection is a popular form of environmental law. Such incentives include pollution taxes, subsidies for clean technologies and practices, and the creation of markets in either environmental protection or pollution. Denmark, The Netherlands, and Sweden, for example, impose taxes on carbon dioxide emissions, and the EU has debated whether to implement such a tax at the supranational level to combat climate change. In the United States, water pollution legislation passed in 1972 provided subsidies to local governments to upgrade publicly owned sewage treatment plants. In 1980 the U.S. government, prompted in part by the national concern inspired by industrial pollution in the Love Canal neighbourhood in Niagara Falls, New York, created a federal "Superfund" that used general revenues and revenue from taxes on petrochemical feedstocks, crude oil, and general corporate income to finance the cleanup of more than 1,000 sites polluted by hazardous substances.

By the 1990s, "tradable allowance schemes," which permit companies to buy and sell "pollution credits," or legal rights to produce specified amounts of pollution, had been implemented in the United States. The most comprehensive and complex such program, created as part of the 1990 Clean Air Act, was designed to reduce overall sulfur dioxide emissions by fossil-fuel-fired power plants. According to proponents, the program would provide financial rewards to cleaner plants, which could sell their unneeded credits on the market, and allow dirtier plants to stay in business while they converted to cleaner technologies.

SET-ASIDE SCHEMES

A final method of environmental protection is the setting aside of lands and waters in their natural state. In the United States, for example, the vast majority of the land owned by the federal government (about one-third of the total land area of the country) can be developed only with the approval of a federal agency. Europe has an extensive network of national parks and preserves on both public and private land, and there are extensive national parks in southern and eastern Africa in which wildlife is protected. Arguably, the large body of law that regulates use of public lands and publicly held resources is "environmental law." Some, however, maintain that it is not.

Many areas of law can be characterized as both "set aside" and regulatory. For example, international efforts to preserve wetlands have focused on setting aside areas of ecological value, including wetlands, and on regulating their use. The Ramsar Convention provides that wetlands are a significant "economic, cultural, scientific and recreational" resource, and a section of the Clean Water Act, the primary U.S. law for the protection of wetlands, contains a prohibition against unpermitted discharges of "dredge and fill material" into any "waters of the United States."

PRINCIPLES OF ENVIRONMENTAL LAW

The design and application of modern environmental law have been shaped by a set of principles and concepts outlined in publications such as *Our Common Future* (1987), published by the World Commission on Environment and Development, and the Earth Summit's Rio Declaration (1992).

THE PRECAUTIONARY PRINCIPLE

Environmental law regularly operates in areas complicated by high levels of scientific uncertainty. In the case of many activities that entail some change to the environment, it is impossible to determine precisely what effects the activity will have on the quality of the environment or on human health. It is generally impossible to know, for example, whether a certain level of air pollution will result in an increase in mortality from respiratory disease, whether a certain level of water pollution will reduce a healthy fish population, or whether oil development in an environmentally sensitive area will significantly disturb the native wildlife. The precautionary principle requires that, if there is a strong suspicion that a certain activity may have environmentally harmful consequences, it is better to control that activity now rather than to wait for incontrovertible scientific evidence.

This principle is expressed in the Rio Declaration, which stipulates that, where there are "threats of serious or irreversible damage, lack of full scientific certainty shall not be used as a reason for postponing cost-effective measures to prevent environmental degradation." In the United States the precautionary principle was incorporated into the design of habitat-conservation plans required under the aegis of the Endangered Species Act. In 1989 the EC invoked the precautionary principle when it banned the importation of U.S. hormone-fed beef, and in 2000 the organization adopted the principle as a "full-fledged and general principle of international law." In 1999 Australia and New Zealand invoked the precautionary principle in their suit against Japan for its alleged overfishing of southern bluefin tuna.

THE PREVENTION PRINCIPLE

Although much environmental legislation is drafted in response to catastrophes, preventing environmental harm is cheaper, easier, and less environmentally dangerous than reacting to environmental harm that already has taken place. The prevention principle is the fundamental notion behind laws regulating the generation, transportation, treatment, storage, and disposal of hazardous waste and laws regulating the use of pesticides. The principle was the foundation of the Basel Convention on the Control of Transboundary Movements of Hazardous Wastes and their Disposal (1989), which sought to minimize the production of hazardous waste and to combat illegal dumping. The prevention principle also was an important element of the EC's Third Environmental Action Programme, which was adopted in 1983.

THE "POLLUTER PAYS" PRINCIPLE

Since the early 1970s the "polluter pays" principle has been a dominant concept in environmental law. Many economists claim that much environmental harm is caused by producers who "externalize" the costs of their activities. For example, factories that emit unfiltered exhaust into the atmosphere or discharge untreated chemicals into a river pay little to dispose of their waste. Instead, the cost of waste disposal in the form of pollution is borne by the entire community. Similarly, the driver of an automobile bears the costs of fuel and maintenance but externalizes the costs associated with the gases emitted from the tailpipe. Accordingly, the purpose of many environmental regulations is to force polluters to bear the real costs of their pollution, though such costs often are difficult to calculate precisely. In theory, such measures encourage producers of pollution to make cleaner products or to use cleaner technologies. The "polluter pays" principle underlies U.S. laws requiring the cleanup of releases of hazardous substances, including oil.

One such law, the Oil Pollution Act (1990), was passed in reaction to the spillage of some 11 million gallons (41 million litres) of oil into Prince William Sound in Alaska in 1989. The "polluter pays" principle also guides the policies of the EU and other governments throughout the world. A 1991 ordinance in Germany, for example, held businesses responsible for the costs of recycling or disposing of their products' packaging, up to the end of the product's life cycle. However, the German Federal Constitutional Court struck down the regulation as unconstitutional. Such policies also have been adopted at the regional or state level; in 1996 the U.S. state of Florida, in order to protect its environmentally sensitive Everglades region, incorporated a limited "polluter pays" provision into its constitution.

THE INTEGRATION PRINCIPLE

Environmental protection requires that due consideration be given to the potential consequences of environmentally fateful decisions. Various jurisdictions (e.g., the United States and the EU) and business organizations (e.g., the U.S. Chamber of Commerce) have integrated environmental considerations into their decision-making processes through environmental-impact-assessment mandates and other provisions.

The Public Participation Principle

Decisions about environmental protection often formally integrate the views of the public. Generally, government decisions to set environmental standards for specific types of pollution, to permit significant environmentally damaging activities, or to preserve significant resources are made only after the impending decision has been formally and publicly announced and the public has been given the opportunity to influence the decision through written comments or hearings. In many countries citizens may challenge in court or before administrative bodies government decisions affecting the environment. These citizen lawsuits have become an important component of environmental decision making at both the national and the international level.

Public participation in environmental decision making has been facilitated in Europe and North America by laws that mandate extensive public access to government information on the environment. Similar measures at the international level include the Rio Declaration and the 1998 Århus Convention, which committed the 40 European signatory states to increase the environmental information available to the public and to enhance the public's ability to participate in government decisions that affect the environment. During the 1990s the Internet became a primary vehicle for disseminating environmental information to the public.

SUSTAINABLE DEVELOPMENT

Sustainable development is an approach to economic planning that attempts to foster economic growth while preserving the quality of the environment for future generations. Despite its enormous popularity in the last two decades of the 20th century, the concept of sustainable development proved difficult to apply in many cases, primarily because the results of long-term sustainability analyses depend on the particular resources focused upon. For example, a forest that will provide a sustained yield of timber in perpetuity may not support native bird populations, and a mineral deposit that will eventually be exhausted may nevertheless support more or less sustainable communities. Sustainability was the focus of the 1992 Earth Summit and later was central to a multitude of environmental studies.

One of the most important areas of the law of sustainable development is ecotourism, which is recreational travel for the purposes of observing and conserving natural environments. Although tourism poses the threat of environmental harm from pollution and the overuse of natural resources, it also can create economic incentives for the preservation of the environment in developing countries and increase awareness of unique and fragile ecosystems throughout the world. In 1995 the World Conference on Sustainable Tourism, held on the island of Lanzarote in the Canary Islands, adopted a charter that encouraged the development of laws that would promote the dual goals of economic development through tourism and protection of the environment. Two years later, in the Malé Declaration on Sustainable Tourism, 27 Asian-Pacific countries pledged themselves to a set of principles that included fostering awareness of environmental ethics in

Tourists gaze at Argentina's Perito Moreno glacier. The Park and National Reservation Los Glaciares, where the glacier resides, has been declared a prime ecotourism destination by UNESCO. Daniel Garcia/AFP/Getty Images

tourism, reducing waste, promoting natural and cultural diversity, and supporting local economies and local community involvement. Highlighting the growing importance of sustainable tourism, the World Tourism Organization declared 2002 the International Year of Ecotourism.

CURRENT TRENDS AND PROSPECTS

Although numerous international environmental treaties have been concluded, effective agreements remain difficult to achieve for a variety of reasons. Because environmental problems ignore political boundaries, they can be adequately addressed only with the cooperation of numerous governments, among which there may be serious disagreements on important points of environmental policy. Furthermore, because the measures necessary to address environmental problems typically result in social and economic hardships in the countries that adopt them, many countries, particularly in the developing world, have been reluctant to enter into environmental treaties. Since the 1970s, a growing number of environmental treaties have incorporated provisions designed to encourage their adoption by developing countries. Such measures include financial cooperation, technology transfer, and differential implementation schedules and obligations.

The greatest challenge to the effectiveness of environmental treaties is compliance. Although treaties can attempt to enforce compliance through mechanisms such as sanctions, such measures usually are of limited usefulness, in part because countries in compliance with a treaty may be unwilling or unable to impose the sanctions called for by the treaty. In general, the threat of sanctions is less important to most countries than the possibility that by violating their international obligations they risk losing their good standing in the international community.

Enforcement mechanisms other than sanctions have been difficult to establish, usually because they would require countries to cede significant aspects of their national sovereignty to foreign or international organizations. In most agreements, therefore, enforcement is treated as a domestic issue, an approach that effectively allows each country to define compliance in whatever way best serves its national interest. Despite this difficulty, international environmental treaties and agreements are likely to grow in importance as international environmental problems become more acute.

Many areas of international environmental law remain underdeveloped. Although international agreements have helped to make the laws and regulations applicable to some types of environmentally harmful activity more or less consistent in different countries, those applicable to other such activities can differ in dramatic ways. Because in most cases the damage caused by environmentally harmful activities cannot be contained within national boundaries, the lack of consistency in the law has led to situations in which activities that are legal in some countries result in illegal or otherwise unacceptable levels of environmental damage in neighbouring countries.

This problem became particularly acute with the adoption of free trade agreements beginning in the early 1990s. The North American Free Trade Agreement (NAFTA), for example, resulted in the creation of large numbers of maquiladoras—factories jointly owned by U.S. and Mexican corporations and operated in Mexico—inside a 100-km- (60-mile) wide free trade zone along the U.S.-Mexican border. Because Mexico's government lacked both the resources and the political will to enforce the country's environmental laws, the maquiladoras were able to pollute surrounding areas with relative impunity, often dumping hazardous wastes on the ground or directly into waterways, where they were carried into U.S. territory.

Prior to NAFTA's adoption in 1992, the prospect of problems such as these led negotiators to append a so-called "side agreement" to the treaty, which pledged environmental cooperation between the signatory states. Meanwhile, in Europe concerns about the apparent connection between free trade agreements and environmental degradation fueled opposition to the Maastricht Treaty, which created the EU and expanded its jurisdiction.

ENVIRONMENTAL ENGINEERING

Environmental engineering develops processes and infrastructure for the supply of water, the disposal of waste, and the control of pollution of all kinds. These endeavours protect public health by preventing disease transmission, and they preserve the quality of the environment by averting the contamination and degradation of air, water, and land resources. Environmental engineering is a field of broad scope that draws on such disciplines as chemistry, ecology, geology, hydraulics, hydrology, microbiology, economics, and mathematics.

Projects in environmental engineering involve the treatment and distribution of drinking water; the collection, treatment, and disposal of wastewater; the control of air pollution and noise pollution; municipal solid-waste management and hazardous-waste management; the cleanup of hazardous-waste sites; and the preparation of environmental assessments, audits, and impact studies. Mathematical modeling and computer analysis are widely used to evaluate and design the systems required for such tasks. Chemical and mechanical engineers may also be involved in the process. Environmental engineering functions include applied research and teaching; project planning and management; the design, construction, and operation of facilities; the sale and marketing of environmental-control equipment; and the enforcement of environmental standards and regulations.

The education of environmental engineers usually involves graduate-level course work, though some colleges and universities allow undergraduates to specialize or take elective courses in the environmental field. Programs offering associate (two-year) degrees are available for training environmental technicians. In the public sector, environmental engineers are employed by national and regional environmental agencies, local health departments, and municipal engineering and public works departments. In the private sector, they are employed by consulting engineering firms, construction contractors, water and sewerage utility companies, and manufacturing industries.

ENVIRONMENTALISM

Environmentalism is described as a political and ethical movement that seeks to improve and protect the quality of the natural environment. Improvement and protection come about through changes to environmentally harmful human activities; the adoption of forms of political, economic, and social organization that are thought to be necessary for, or at least conducive to, the benign treatment of the environment by humans; and a reassessment of humanity's relationship with nature. In various ways, environmentalism claims that living things other than humans, and the natural environment as a whole, are deserving of consideration in reasoning about the morality of political, economic, and social policies.

INTELLECTUAL UNDERPINNINGS

Environmental thought and the various branches of the environmental movement are often classified into two intellectual camps: those that are considered anthropocentric, or "human-centred," in orientation and those considered biocentric, or "life-centred." This division has been described in other terminology as "shallow" ecology versus "deep" ecology and as "technocentrism" versus "ecocentrism."

Anthropocentric approaches focus mainly on the negative effects that environmental degradation has on human beings and their interests, including their interests in health, recreation, and quality of life. It is often characterized by a mechanistic approach to nonhuman nature in which individual creatures and species have only an instrumental value for humans. The defining feature of anthropocentrism is that it considers the moral obligations humans have to the environment to derive from obligations that humans have to each other—and, less crucially, to future generations of humans—rather than from any obligation to other living things or to the environment as a whole. Human obligations to the environment are thus indirect.

Critics of anthropocentrism have charged that it amounts to a form of human "chauvinism." They argue that anthropocentric approaches presuppose the historically Western view of nature as merely a resource to be managed or exploited for human purposes—a view that they claim is responsible for centuries of environmental destruction. In contrast to anthropocentrism, biocentrism claims that nature has an intrinsic moral worth that does not depend on its usefulness to human beings, and it is this intrinsic worth that gives rise directly to obligations to the environment. Humans are therefore morally bound to protect the environment, as well as individual creatures and species, for their own sake. In this sense, biocentrics view human beings and other elements of the natural environment, both living and often nonliving, as members of a single moral and ecological community.

By the 1960s and '70s, as scientific knowledge of the causes and consequences of environmental degradation was becoming more extensive and sophisticated, there was increasing concern among some scientists, intellectuals, and activists about the Earth's ability to absorb the detritus of human economic activity and, indeed, to sustain human life. This concern contributed to the growth of grassroots environmental activism in a number of countries, the establishment of new environmental nongovernmental organizations, and the formation of environmental ("green") political parties in a number of Western democracies. As political leaders gradually came to appreciate the seriousness of environmental problems, governments entered into negotiations in the early 1970s that led to the adoption of a growing number of international environmental agreements.

The division between anthropocentric and biocentric approaches played a central role in the development of environmental thought in the late 20th century. Whereas some earlier schools, such as apocalyptic (survivalist) environmentalism and emancipatory environmentalism—as well as its offshoot, human-welfare ecology—were animated primarily by a concern for human well-being, later movements, including social ecology, deep ecology, the animal-rights and animal-liberation movements, and ecofeminism, were centrally concerned with the moral worth of nonhuman nature.

ANTHROPOCENTRIC SCHOOLS OF THOUGHT

The vision of the environmental movement of the 1960s and early '70s was generally pessimistic, reflecting a pervasive sense of "civilization malaise" and a conviction that the Earth's long-term prospects were bleak. Works such as Rachel Carson's *Silent Spring* (1962), Garrett Hardin's "The Tragedy of the Commons" (1968), Paul Ehrlich's *The Population Bomb* (1968), Donella H. Meadows' *The Limits to Growth* (1972), and Edward Goldsmith's *Blueprint for Survival* (1972) suggested that the planetary ecosystem was reaching the limits of what it could sustain.

This so-called apocalyptic, or survivalist, literature encouraged reluctant calls from some environmentalists for increasing the powers of centralized governments over human activities deemed environmentally harmful, a viewpoint expressed most vividly in Robert Heilbroner's *An Inquiry into the Human Prospect* (1974), which argued that human survival ultimately required the sacrifice of human freedom. Counterarguments, such as those presented in Julian Simon and Herman Kahn's *The Resourceful Earth* (1984), emphasized humanity's ability to find or to invent substitutes for resources that were scarce and in danger of being exhausted.

Beginning in the 1970s many environmentalists attempted to develop strategies for limiting environmental degradation through recycling, the use of alternative-energy technologies, the decentralization and democratization of economic and social planning, and, for some, a reorganization of major industrial sectors, including the agriculture and energy industries. In contrast to apocalyptic environmentalism, so-called "emancipatory" environmentalism took a more positive and practical approach, one aspect of which was the effort to promote an ecological consciousness and an ethic of "stewardship" of the environment. One form of emancipatory environmentalism, human-welfare ecology—which aims to enhance human life by creating a safe and clean environment—was part of a broader concern with distributive justice and reflected the tendency, later characterized as "postmaterialist," of citizens in advanced industrial societies to place more importance on "quality-of-life" issues than on traditional economic concerns.

Emancipatory environmentalism also was distinguished for some of its advocates by an emphasis on developing small-scale systems of economic production that would be more closely integrated with the natural processes of surrounding ecosystems. This more environmentally holistic approach to economic planning was promoted in work by the American ecologist Barry Commoner and by the German economist Ernst Friedrich Schumacher. In contrast to earlier thinkers who had downplayed the interconnectedness of natural systems, Commoner and Schumacher emphasized productive processes that worked with nature, not against it, encouraged the use of organic and renewable resources rather than synthetic products (e.g., plastics and chemical fertilizers), and advocated renewable and small-scale energy resources (e.g., wind and solar power) and government policies that supported effective public transportation and energy efficiency. The emancipatory approach was evoked through the 1990s in the popular slogan, "Think globally, act locally." Its small-scale, decentralized planning and production has been criticized, however, as unrealistic in highly urbanized and industrialized societies.

BIOCENTRIC SCHOOLS OF THOUGHT

An emphasis on small-scale economic structures and the social dimensions of the ecological crisis also is a feature of the school of thought known as social ecology, whose major proponent was the American environmental anarchist Murray Bookchin. Social ecologists trace the causes of environmental degradation to the existence of unjust, hierarchical relationships in human society, which they see as endemic to the large-scale social structures of modern capitalist states. Accordingly, they argue, the most environmentally sympathetic form of political and social organization is one based on decentralized small-scale communities and systems of production.

A more radical doctrine, known as deep ecology, builds on preservationist themes from the early environmental movement. Its main originators, the Norwegian philosopher Arne Næss, the American sociologist Bill Devall, and the American philosopher George Sessions, share with social ecologists a distrust of capitalism and industrial technology and favour decentralized forms of social organization. Deep ecologists also claim that humans need to regain a "spiritual" relationship with nonhuman nature. By understanding the interconnectedness of all organisms—including humans—in the ecosphere and empathizing with nonhuman nature, they argue, humans would develop an ecological consciousness and a sense of ecological solidarity. The biocentric principle of interconnectedness was extensively developed by British environmentalist James Lovelock, who postulated in *Gaia: A New Look at Life on Earth* (1979) that the planet is a single living, self-regulating entity capable of reestablishing an ecological equilibrium, even without the existence of human life. Despite their emphasis on spirituality, some more extreme forms of deep ecology have been strongly criticized as antihumanist, on the ground that they entail opposition to famine relief and immigration and acceptance of large-scale losses of life caused by AIDS and other pandemics.

The emphasis on intrinsic value and the interconnectedness of nature was fundamental to the development of the animal-rights movement, whose activism was influenced by works such as Peter Singer's *Animal Liberation* (1977) and Tom Regan's *The Case for Animal Rights* (1983). Animal rights approaches go beyond a concern with illtreatment and cruelty to animals, demanding an end to all forms of animal exploitation, including the use of animals in scientific and medical experiments and as sources of entertainment (e.g., in circuses, rodeos, and races) and food.

Oppression, hierarchy, and spiritual relationships with nature also have been central concerns of ecofeminism. Ecofeminists assert that there is a connection between the destruction of nature by humans and the oppression of women by men that arises from political theories and social practices in which both women and nature are treated as objects to be owned or controlled. Ecofeminists aim to establish a central role for women in the pursuit of an environmentally sound and socially just society. They have been divided, however, over how to conceive of the relationship between nature and women, which they hold is more intimate and more "spiritual" than the relationship between nature and men. Whereas cultural ecofeminists argue that the relationship is inherent in women's reproductive and nurturing roles, social ecofeminists, while acknowledging the relationship's immediacy, claim that it arises from social and cultural hierarchies that confine women primarily to the private sphere.

HISTORY OF THE ENVIRONMENTAL MOVEMENT

Concern for the impact on human life of problems such as air and water pollution dates to at least Roman times. Pollution was associated with the spread of epidemic disease in Europe between the late 14th century and the mid

16th century, and soil conservation was practiced in China, India, and Peru as early as 2,000 years ago. In general, however, such concerns did not give rise to public activism.

The contemporary environmental movement arose primarily from concerns in the late 19th century about the protection of the countryside in Europe and the wilderness in the United States and the health consequences of pollution during the Industrial Revolution. In opposition to the dominant political philosophy of the time, liberalism—which held that all social problems, including environmental ones, could and should be solved through the free market—most early environmentalists believed that government rather than the market should be charged with protecting the environment and ensuring the conservation of resources. An early philosophy of resource conservation was developed by Gifford Pinchot (1865–1946), the first chief of the U.S. Forest Service, for whom conservation represented the wise and efficient use of resources. Also in the United States at about the same time, a more strongly biocentric approach arose in the preservationist philosophy of John Muir (1838–1914), founder of the Sierra Club, and Aldo Leopold (1887–1948), a professor of wildlife management who was pivotal in the designation of Gila National Forest in New Mexico in 1924 as America's first national wilderness area. Leopold introduced the concept of a land ethic, arguing that humans should transform themselves from conquerors of nature into citizens of it; his essays, compiled posthumously in *A Sand County Almanac* (1949), had a significant influence on later biocentric environmentalists.

Environmental organizations established from the late 19th to the mid 20th century were primarily middle-class lobbying groups concerned with nature conservation, wildlife protection, and the pollution that arose from industrial development and urbanization. There were also scientific organizations concerned with natural history and with biological aspects of conservation efforts.

Beginning in the 1960s the various philosophical strands of environmentalism were given political expression through the establishment of "green" political movements in the form of activist nongovernmental organizations and environmentalist political parties. Despite the diversity of the environmental movement, four pillars provided a unifying theme to the broad goals of political ecology: protection of the environment, grassroots democracy, social justice, and nonviolence. However, for a small number of environmental groups and individual activists who engaged in ecoterrorism, violence was viewed as a justified response to what they considered the violent treatment of nature by some interests, particularly the logging and mining industries. The political goals of the contemporary green movement in the industrialized West focused on changing government policy and promoting environmental social values. In the less-industrialized or developing world, environmentalism has been more closely involved in "emancipatory" politics and grassroots activism on issues such as poverty, democratization, and political and human rights, including the rights of women and indigenous peoples. Examples of such movements include the Chipko movement in India, which linked forest protection with the rights of women, and the Assembly of the Poor in Thailand, a coalition of movements fighting for the right to participate in environmental and development policies.

The early strategies of the contemporary environmental movement were self-consciously activist and unconventional, involving direct-protest actions designed to obstruct and to draw attention to environmentally harmful policies and projects. Other strategies included public-education and media campaigns, community-directed activities, and conventional lobbying of policy makers and political representatives. The movement also attempted to set public examples in order to increase awareness of and sensitivity to environmental issues. Such projects included recycling, green consumerism (also known as "buying green"), and the establishment of alternative communities, including self-sufficient farms, workers' cooperatives, and cooperative-housing projects.

The electoral strategies of the environmental movement included the nomination of environmental candidates and the registration of green political parties. These parties were conceived of as a new kind of political organization that would bring the influence of the grass-roots environmental movement directly to bear on the machinery of government, make the environment a central concern of public policy, and render the institutions of the state more democratic, transparent, and accountable. The world's first green parties — the Values Party, a nationally based party in New Zealand, and the United Tasmania Group, organized in the Australian state of Tasmania — were founded in the early 1970s. The first explicitly green member of a national legislature was elected in Switzerland in 1979; later, in 1981, four greens won legislative seats in Belgium. Green parties also have been formed in the former Soviet bloc, where they were instrumental in the collapse of some communist regimes, and in some developing countries in Asia, South America, and Africa, though they have achieved little electoral success there.

The most successful environmental party has been the German Green Party (die Grünen), founded in 1980. Although it failed to win representation in federal elections that year, it entered the Bundestag (parliament) in both 1983 and 1987, winning 5.6 percent and 8.4 percent of the national vote, respectively. The party did not win representation in 1990, but in 1998 it formed a governing coalition with the Social Democratic Party, and the party's leader, Joschka Fischer, was appointed as the country's foreign minister. Throughout the last two decades of the 20th century, green parties won national representation in a number of countries and even claimed the office of mayor in European capital cities such as Dublin and Rome in the mid-1990s.

By this time green parties had become broad political vehicles, though they continued to focus on the environment. In developing party policy, they attempted to apply the values of environmental philosophy to all issues facing their countries, including foreign policy, defense, and social and economic policies.

Despite the success of some environmental parties, environmentalists remained divided over the ultimate value of electoral politics. For some, participation in elections is essential because it increases the public's awareness of environmental issues and encourages traditional political parties to address them. Others, however, have argued that the compromises necessary for electoral success invariably undermine the ethos of grassroots democracy and direct action. This tension was perhaps most pronounced in the German Green Party. The party's *Realos* (realists) accepted the need for coalitions and compromise with other political parties, including traditional parties with views sometimes contrary to that of the Green Party. By contrast, the *Fundis* (fundamentalists) maintained that direct action should remain the major form of political action and that no pacts or alliances should be formed with other parties. Likewise, in Britain, where the Green Party achieved success in some local elections but failed to win representation at the national level (though it did win 15 percent of the vote in the 1989 European

Greenpeace activists hang a banner calling for several world leaders to take action on climate change during a 2009 demonstration in Manaus, Brazil. Rodrigo Baleia/LatinContent/Getty Images

Parliament elections), this tension was evidenced in disputes between so-called "electoralists" and "radicals."

The implementation of internal party democracy also caused fissures within environmental parties. In particular, earlier strategies such as continuous policy involvement by party members, grassroots control over all party institutions and decisions, and the legislative rotation of elected members to prevent the creation of career politicians were sometimes perceived as unhelpful and disruptive when green parties won representation to local, national, or regional assemblies.

By the late 1980s environmentalism had become a global as well as a national political force. Some environmental nongovernmental organizations (e.g., Greenpeace, Friends of the Earth, and the World Wildlife Fund) established a significant international presence, with offices throughout the world and centralized international headquarters to coordinate lobbying campaigns and to serve as campaign centres and information clearinghouses for their national affiliate organizations. Transnational coalition building was and remains another important strategy for environmental organizations and for grassroots movements in developing countries, primarily because it facilitates the exchange of information and expertise but also because it strengthens lobbying and direct-action campaigns at the international level.

Through its international activism, the environmental movement has influenced the agenda of international politics. Although a small number of bilateral and multilateral international environmental agreements were in force before the 1960s, since the 1972 United Nations Conference on the Human Environment in Stockholm, the variety of multilateral environmental agreements has increased to cover most aspects of environmental protection as well as many practices with environmental consequences, such as the trade in endangered species, the management of hazardous waste, especially nuclear waste, and armed conflict. The changing nature of public debate on the environment was reflected also in the organization of the 1992 United Nations Conference on Environment and Development (the Earth Summit) in Rio de Janeiro, Brazil, which was attended by representatives from some 180 countries and various business groups, nongovernmental organizations, and the media. In the 21st century, the environmental movement has combined the traditional concerns of conservation, preservation, and pollution with more contemporary concerns with the environmental consequences of economic practices as diverse as tourism, trade, financial investment, and the conduct of war. Environmentalists are likely to intensify the trends of the late 20th century, during which some environmental groups increasingly worked in coalition not just with other emancipatory organizations, such as human rights and indigenous-peoples groups, but also with corporations and other businesses.

CONCLUSION

In late 2007, the UN Environment Programme (UNEP) published its fourth global environment outlook assessment. It warned that climate change, the loss of biodiversity, and land degradation were among the greatest challenges facing the world. UNEP director Achim Steiner said in a statement that "the systematic destruction of the Earth's natural and nature-based resources has reached a point where the economic viability of economies is being challenged—and where the bill we hand on to our children may prove impossible to pay."

That same year, however, the Asahi Glass Foundation awarded two Blue Planet Prizes, each worth more than

$400,000, to Americans Joseph L. Sax and Amory B. Lovins. Sax was honoured for drafting the world's first modern environmental law to be based on public-trust doctrine—it supported citizen action for environmental protection—and for establishing environmental laws internationally. Lovins was rewarded for his contributions to the protection of the environment through the improved energy efficiency advocated by his "soft energy path" and for his invention of an ultralight and fuel-efficient vehicle called the Hypercar. The following year the Blue Prize went to Claude Lorius, director emeritus of research at the French National Center for Scientific Research, for work on calculating ancient levels of atmospheric carbon dioxide from Antarctic ice cores, and to the University of São Paulo's José Goldemberg, who helped launch Brazil's bioethanol program in the 1970s. The 2009 Blue Planet Prize went to Hirofumi Uzawa of Japan and Nicholas Stern of the U.K. Uzawa was honoured for his advocacy of the concept of social common capital as a theoretical framework for confronting environmental issues. Lord Stern was recognized for his report "The Economics of Climate Change," which he prepared for the U.K. government.

Honours and awards such as the Blue Planet Prize are a tangible sign that a large body of people are well aware of the potential destruction of our natural environment and are working with dedication to prevent it. The list of challenges is long, but the technology to deal with it exists, as do the intelligence and, in growing numbers of people, the will. It is in the combination of these three assets—technology, intelligence, and will—that the key to controlling and reversing pollution lies. This book has described areas where the wise application of technology has already begun to work. One can be confident that the work will continue, for the human species has no other choice.

GLOSSARY

acid rain Precipitation with inordinately low pH levels
and, thereby, high acidic content, created when the
water vapour in clouds is mixed with gases from fossil
fuel emissions.

afterburner A special incineration unit made of refractory materials housed in a steel shell; used to convert
harmful gases into carbon dioxide and water.

anaerobic Capable of sustained life without oxygen.

anthropocentrism Viewing the world in a way that only
takes into account human values.

anthropogenic Originating from human activities.

aquifer An underground geologic formation that acts as
a natural catch basin for water; a water-bearing layer
of earth.

carbon sequestration Long-term carbon retention by
plants, soil, or water, which can occur naturally or as
the result of human activity.

cullet Used, broken, or flawed glass that has been designated as refuse that can be recycled.

desalination A water treatment method that involves
the separation of fresh water from salt water or
brackish water.

estuary A section of coastal water that contains fresh
and salt water, and is partly enclosed by land.

eutrophication The gradual accumulation of plant
nutrients in a relatively sedentary body of water, such
as a lake.

flocculation Separating solid particles from a liquid,
resulting in clusters of soft, flaky material.

fly ash The soot, dust, and cinders generated as material is incinerated, or burned.

gyre A system of ocean currents that spirals around a central zone.

hydrologic cycle The continuous circulation of water through Earth's atmosphere, surface, and oceans.

hydrocarbons An organic compound of hydrogen and carbon, the principal component of fossil fuels.

leachate The contaminated liquid created when decomposing garbage mixes with precipitation.

nonputrescible Not liable to putrefy, or become rotten.

oligotrophic Lacking in plant nutrients yet typically rich in dissolved oxygen.

particulates Small fragments of solid material or liquid droplets that are suspended in air.

photochemical smog A haze in the air caused when sunlight reacts with nitrogen and hydrocarbon emissions from, primarily, automobiles.

potable Water or other liquid that is fit for human consumption.

radiative forcing The measurable influence of climatic factors on the amount of radiant energy impinging upon Earth's surface; as defined by the Intergovernmental Panel on Climate Change.

reactive waste Chemically unstable refuse that reacts violently with air or water; a type of hazardous waste.

refuse cell A section of a sanitary landfill reserved for the task of spreading and compacting refuse, so that it may be covered with a layer of soil.

subsidence The sinking of Earth's surface in response to geologic or anthropogenic causes.

Superfund A United States government fund set aside to pay for cleanup after hazardous-waste spills.

temperature inversion A condition in which a layer of cool air is overlain by a layer of warm air, and the atmosphere is very stable.

turbidity The degree of cloudiness caused by particles from organic and inorganic substances suspended in water.

watershed A land area in which all precipitation flows into a single river system.

windrow A long mound of organic refuse that is turned into compost when tended.

xenobiotic Inorganic chemicals that are considered harmful soil pollutants.

FOR FURTHER READING

Andrady, Anthony L. Plastics and the Environment.
    Malden, MA: Wiley InterScience, 2003.
Benedickson, Jamie, and Winn, Graeme. The Culture
    of Flushing: A Social and Legal History of Sewage.
    Vancouver, B.C.: University of British Columbia
    Press, 2007.
Bhatia, S.C. Textbook of Noise Pollution and Its Control.
    New Delhi, India: Atlantic Publishers and
    Distributors, 2007.
Carson, Rachel. Silent Spring. Orlando, FL: Mariner Books
    (a division of Houghton Mifflin Harcourt), 2002.
Colls, Jeremy, and Tiwary, Abhishek. Air Pollution:
    Measurement, Modelling and Mitigation. New York,
    NY: Routledge, 2009.
Cunningham, Mary Ann and William P., and
    Woodworth Saigo, Barbara. Environmental
    Science: A Global Concern. Columbus, OH:
    McGraw-Hill, 2009.
Durant, Darrin, and Fuji Johnson, Genevieve. Nuclear
    Waste Management in Canada: Critical Issues,
    Critical Perspectives. Vancouver, B.C.: University of
    British Columbia Press, 2009.
Hill, Marquita K. Understanding Environmental
    Pollution: A Primer. Cambridge, UK: Cambridge
    University Press, 2004.
Jacobs, Chip, and Kelly, William. Smogtown: The Lung-
    Burning History of Pollution in Los Angeles.
    Woodstock, NY: Overlook Press, 2008.
Jacobson, Mark Z. Atmospheric Pollution. Cambridge,
    UK: Cambridge University Press, 2002.

Kallen, Stuart A. Nuclear and Toxic Waste. Farmington Hills, MI: Greenhaven Press, 2005.

Kosko, Bart. Noise. New York, NY: The Viking Press, 2006.

Nathanson, Jerry A. Basic Environmental Technology: Water Supply, Waste Management and Pollution Control. Upper Saddle River, NJ: Prentice Hall, 2008.

Rich, Catherine, and Longcore, Travis, eds. Ecological Consequences of Artificial Night Lighting. Washington, D.C.: Island Press, 2005.

Royte, Elizabeth. Garbage Land: On the Trail of Trash. Boston, MA: Back Bay Books (Hachette), 2006.

Singal, S.P. Noise Pollution and Control Strategy. Oxford, UK: Alpha Science International, 2005.

Stookes, Paul. A Practical Approach to Environmental Law. New York, NY: Oxford University Press, 2009.

Takashi Asano, et al. Water Reuse: Issues, Technologies, and Applications. New York, NY: McGraw-Hill Professional, 2007.

Vigil, Kenneth G. Clean Water: An Introduction to Water Quality and Pollution Control. Corvallis, OR: Oregon State University Press, 2003.

Watson, Stephanie, ed. Critical Perspectives on Pollution. New York, NY: Rosen Publishing Group, 2007

INDEX